Writing in the Margins

Praise for *Writing in the Margins*

"May I really write words and draw pictures in the margins of my Bible?" (My Bible has some underlinings and a few hesitant pencil or erasable chalk punctuation marks.) In her lovely and liberating book, Lisa Hickman not only says, "Yes!" but she hands out permission slips to pick up our writing tools and go for it. With stories of people whose Bible margins are filled with notes and doodles, and with simple exercises to get started, Lisa encourages us to physically engage the Word of the Living God, not just worship an ancient book.

—Sybil MacBeth, author of *Praying in Color: Drawing a New Path to God*

One of the gifts of this book is "On the Pages of Your Bible"—deep questions that invite our deep thinking, instructions that lead to reflection and wonderment, encouragements that draw out our true and truer selves. Rather than fearing you won't know what to write, fear instead you will discover too much of who you are. Then, "Fear not," for Lisa Nichols Hickman shows us that in discovering ourselves, we discover God.

—Joyce MacKichan Walker, Minister of Education at Nassau Presbyterian Church in Princeton, NJ, is a teacher, keynoter, curriculum writer, and the 2008 Educator of the Year for the Association of Presbyterian Church Educators

In her book, *Writing in the Margins*, Lisa Hickman carries her readers to a fresh and intimate engagement with the words of scripture though a deep conversation with the text in the margins of the Bible that will then spill out into transformed lives. Hickman draws upon the same energy that is present in young adulthood and coaxes us into a lifetime of deep engagement with scripture. In a world where life often takes us to the margins, in one way or another, Hickman's text is inspired and provocative, and it brings new and creative vitality to the biblical witness.

—Pastor Mary Brown, editor of "ON Scripture—The Bible," Odyssey Network

In the first book of the Bible, Jacob, a conniving protagonist, wrestles with God at midnight. As the sun glimpses over the horizon, God leaves Jacob with a wrenched hip and a blessing. In *Writing in the Margins*, Lisa Hickman invites us into that holy struggle. As we learn to grapple, the words, stories, and disciplines in this book will leave us broken and blessed.

—Carol Howard Merritt, author of *Tribal Church* and *Reframing Hope*

After reading a few pages of Lisa Nichols Hickman's *Writing in the Margins*, I got up off the couch to hunt for a pencil and my Bible. She led me into a hidden world of other Christians' relationships with God through scripture in a way that lures me back into a love affair with the book. Her stories are nothing we have heard before; her questions in each chapter invite true discovery. Nothing trite here. She invites us into the practice of relating to the Bible in a fresh, unique, and compelling way that welcomes both newcomers and old-timers.

—Melissa Wiginton serves as Vice President for Education Beyond the Walls at Austin Presbyterian Theological Seminary in Austin, Texas

Not only does Lisa Hickman give her readers a remarkably simple yet rich spiritual practice; in a book that is purportedly about the white space framing sacred scripture, she offers deeply moving biblical reflections. Ironically, *Writing in the Margins* will play a central role in the life of many contemporary Christians.

—Katherine Willis Pershey, author of *Any Day a Beautiful Change: A Story of Faith and Family*

Talk about a book that practices what it preaches. *Writing in the Margins* not only opens the door to new thinking about the spiritual practice of journaling, but it, literally, gives you space to do just that. From the eloquence of Hickman's thoughtful prose to the depth of her theological musings, I'm certain that all those who settle down with this book will find themselves captivated by her words of wisdom and inspired by her passion.

— Jason Santos, author of *A Community Called Taizé: A Story of Prayer, Worship and Reconciliation*

Lisa Hickman makes the luminous claim in *Writing in the Margins* that decisive action takes place not in the marks of the Bible's text but in the voids beside the text. She challenges the reader to meet the Word in those pristine spaces, with minds alert, imaginations attuned, and pencil in hand. For Hickman, the Bible's margins, as with the margins of life, form the terrain of the Spirit.

—Donald Ottenhoff, Executive Director of the Collegeville Institute for Ecumenical and Cultural Research

Before opening this book, I thought it would be about how to read the Bible. Then I discovered it is really about how to pray. I shouldn't have been surprised; those two things go hand in hand.

—Matthew L. Skinner, Associate Professor of New Testament, Luther Seminary

Informative, practical, and permission-giving. As one who has marked up his Bible for years, it is good to be affirmed in this endeavor and discover other creative ways people of faith are using the margins of the Bible.

—Dan Thomas, Associate Pastor for Education and Nurture, Immanuel Presbyterian Church

Writing in the Margins is a lovely, practical meditation on how to read—no, more than that, how to interact and *be alive with*—Scripture. Which means it gives insight for being alive to faith and to doubt, to answers and to questions, to prayer and to engagement in the world.

—Kent Annan, author of *After Shock* and *Following Jesus Through the Eye of the Needle* and co-director of Haiti Partners

With this lovely reflection on the practice of writing in the margins of our Bibles, Hickman offers a vibrant way to bring the sacred text to life and into our lives. Invoking the wisdom of other gifted margin-writers, she convinces us to take up a pen and join our words with God's Word.

—Maureen R. O'Brien, Ph.D., Associate Professor of Theology, Duquesne University, Pittsburgh, PA

If you're like me—reminiscent about a past when the Spirit burned in your heart and the Word fed your belly—Hickman's book is for you. *Writing in the Margins* lit a new spark of hope and possibility inside me. Thank you, Lisa, for this gift.

—Margot Starbuck, author of *The Girl in the Orange Dress*

Lisa NICHOLS HICKMAN

Writing in the Margins

Connecting with God on the Pages of Your Bible

Abingdon Press

NASHVILLE

WRITING IN THE MARGINS
Connecting with God on the Pages of Your Bible

Library of Congress Cataloging-in-Publication Data

Hickman, Lisa Nichols.
 Writing in the margins : connecting with God on the pages of your Bible / Lisa Nichols
Hickman.
  pages cm
  ISBN 978-1-4267-6750-0 (pbk. : alk. paper) 1. Bible--Reading. 2. Spiritual journals--
Authorship. 3. Bible--Criticism, interpretation, etc. I. Title.
 BS617.H48 2013
 220.6'1--dc23

                                                                    2013013070

13 14 15 16 17 18 19 20 21 22—10 9 8 7 6 5 4 3 2 1

MANUFACTURED IN THE UNITED STATES OF AMERICA

For Rich Gordon and his girls:
Jennifer, Jessica, Megan, and Katie.

The word of Christ must live in you richly.
—Colossians 3:16

CONTENTS

FOREWORD

You have picked up this book. Now you've got to pick up your pen. This is a book that you will underline, dog-ear, and mark up. It is, as they say in this digital age, interactive. You will enjoy it, you will learn interesting things, and you will be inspired. I assure you, if you do interact with it as it invites you to, enjoying the sidebars and pull quotes, and especially doing the exercises and responding to the reflection question, you will live differently as a result. You will start doing this with your Bible. Soon, your whole life will become interactive.

It starts with a holy longing. Or at least curiosity. You've got the book in your hands, so you are partway there. But there is some work to be done. If you are curious, you've got to participate. This is experiential education. Get on those safety goggles, friends. This could get dangerous.

Sociologists and cultural critics (and educators, booksellers, pastors, and all sorts of book lovers) have spilled much ink in recent years about the effect of the internet on our reading habits. Nicholas Carr, in his must-read book *The Shallows,* famously asked, "Is Google making us dumb?" He documents a scary thesis: the interactive and short-form style of online reading has eroded our ability to sustain serious thought, to focus, to think deeply about the printed page (electronic or otherwise.) Perhaps it is emblematic of this problem that the device we use to get to our fast-paced, hot-wired snippets of reading is called a *browser*.

Good readers—and those who value thoughtful interaction with books and the beauty and ideas they carry— know that we have to do more in our study (and more in our lives) than just browse. To put it simply, we have to pay attention. Lisa Nichols Hickman is subversive in this info-glut, zippy age because she invites us to settle down. She invites us to focus. She asks us to care enough to take our learning seriously by refusing to be passive, starting with the printed page and, as the habit is learned, in our very lives.

Close, engaged reading, with pen in hand, paying attention to the words on the page—in any book, although her focus is on the Bible—demands that we do at least two things, and Lisa wisely helps us learn both.

First, we must resist distraction. We have to pay attention to the text. In story after inspirational story, Lisa tells of people she knows who have done this. From a college student involved in a summer beach ministry (and working at a yogurt shop called Peace, Love, and Yogurt – how cool is that?), to a seasoned social activist, to one of the heroes of the book—a middle-aged friend in her congregation who was dying of cancer—she inspires us to learn how to read the Bible carefully. I am sure it will help you see the words on the page with attentiveness. As you've surely already deduced, she helps you learn to do this through the simple art of using that pen. Underline, circle, star, highlight—and write in the margins! If you're nervous about this practice, take comfort in her explanation that it is "consecration, not desecration." She does a fantastic spin on the famous call to read the Bible with the newspaper in the other hand; she says to read the Bible with your pen in the other hand.

But the second thing, after using pen or pencil as a tool to help you focus and see the text in all its strange and glorious wonder, is this: Lisa teaches us to make connections. She tells us, as she looks at the well-worn Bibles of the people in her book, that they have drawn lines and arrows, circled words and then pointed to other words they scribbled. Sometimes there are symbols or dates or exclamation points. They are, almost literally, connecting the dots. Hickman calls them "sacred connections."

And here is the amazing part, something this book will help you with: by writing our own thoughts, feelings, frustrations, and hopes next to the holy text, we discern the connections between God's Word and our lives. By commending this practice, Hickman shows that biblical faith is a living faith. That is, we who are called to be God's people are invited to know God, to listen to God speak, to relate timeless truths from the Bible to the complexities and messiness of our real lives. She swipes a line from the feisty radical historian Studs Turkel, who often told people to write in the margins of the books they read—even to question and disagree!—and thereby to enter into what he called a "raucous conversation" with the author. When the book is as grand and vital as the Bible, and the authors include an array of women and men from several cultures and distant centuries, this interaction is going to be raucous indeed. By inviting us to write in the margins of our Bibles, Lisa helps us enter into this dialogue not only with its inspired truths but also, ultimately, with the Triune God of the universe.

In *Writing in the Margins* you will find all sorts of interesting stuff about writing, books, the history of marginalia (it's a pretty cool word, isn't it?), and what we can learn by being willing to write in our Bibles. Do you know what Elvis wrote in his Bible? Did you know that hundreds of years ago printers figured out a "golden ratio of page design" that helps the eye settle on the text? You know what normal margins are, but did you know the center ones are called gutters?

She doesn't overwork the image, but you can take it from there: sometimes we find God's truth in the gutter, deep in the center of dark hardship where there is little margin and where perhaps even God feels absent. Hickman does not advise us to pick and choose the parts of the Bible that we most like, scribbling up only the sweet stuff. God is a real conversation partner, and the history of redemption unfolds in the full drama of Scripture through thick and thin. As you make connections between the true stories, poems, prayers, politics, songs, and letters that make up the Bible, and the true stuff of your own life—by writing in the margins pieces of your story, the thick and thin of your life—you will, she promises, come to know God's grace in Christ Jesus, the living Word of the words.

Jesus, we all know (or do we?), raised a ruckus in his own holy life. He embraced those on the margins of society, insisted that his own ministry was an inauguration of the ancient Hebrew Year of Jubilee as described in (get this) Leviticus. Lisa starts this study of writing in the margins of the Bible in Leviticus, with a rumination of how God commanded the Israelites to leave margin in their rows of crops, a public agricultural policy that made room for the homeless and poor—those on the margins. It's a good place to start a book, since it is where Jesus started. His very first sermon (recorded in Luke 4, a passage marked up in my own Bible) cites a prophetic text from Isaiah that alludes to Leviticus 25. Jesus, the Lord of the marginalized, preaches about margins, declaring himself to be the one to bring Jubilee shalom to the people of Israel. They liked that, Luke tells us, until Jesus preaches a bit more, suggesting that there are others—non-Jews and enemies!—who get in on God's redemptive regime. He makes some connections, drawing on the margins of Israel's story, and at that point, they want to kill him.

What might you write in the margins of this amazing passage? Will you connect the identity and mission of Jesus with the Old Testament law and prophets? There is good news, indeed, but it may be troubling. Outsiders—those on the margins of society and of our own lives—are included? Grace is bigger than we thought? God cares about the world, about land and prisoners, about justice and restoring all aspects of culture? And we are recruited to be involved in it all? Holy things happen when we inhabit these margins, when we allow the echoes and resonances to come to the fore and to come alive in our lives. You will experience God in fresh and holy ways, through the Bible itself, as you enter the conversation—writing, scribbling, and interacting.

Maybe this practice will be hard for those of us who think that Christian truths are abstract, religious ideals from a gilded-edged Book that are just there. And we must simply agree with them and try hard to live them. This is, you will soon figure out, not the view of the Bible that the Bible itself teaches. Scripture comes to us as a story, which points to a living relationship with a living Lord. It is not static, and it must be embodied anew in each generation, in each life.

Perhaps this practice will come more naturally to those who have grown up digital, interacting with video games and handheld devices. Choose Your Own Adventure books were popular a few years back, and the generation raised to actually enter stories—to help live out the story—might get this high-def way of engaging the Scriptures.

Younger or older, rationalist or experientially inclined, this is a book for us all. It will help us read our Bibles more playfully, even as it teaches us to take it more reflectively; it will deepen our relationship with God and cause us to take our lives more seriously. As we write in the margins, we are entering into a holy space, and as we find God there, we will be slowly shaped into the image of the Christ who embraced those on the margins. This is not magic, and it is not a simple technique. It is a way of life, including habits of reading well, seeking God, and learning to listen. Interacting with the Word of the Lord through Scripture in this scribbling way lays bare our own lives. Over time we are transformed, so that we might be faithful agents of God's reign in the world.

Any book that can help us do this, that can help us make sacred connections between the Word and the world, that can train us to enter this redemptive project of God's rescue of the world, is well worth having. More, it is worth interacting with. Write in the margins of *Writing in the Margins*, and soon you will be writing in the one-inch margins of your Bible. And who knows what will come next? I am sure it will be a holy adventure.

—Byron K. Borger
Hearts & Minds independent bookstore
Dallastown, Pennsylvania

SACRED
EDGES

To live sacred lives requires that we live
at the edge of what we do not know.

—*Anne Hillman*

Blank Spaces

The invitation of this book is, at its simplest, to pick up a pen and write in the blank spaces of your Bible.

It is an invitation to look at the blank spaces of your biblical text and see in the margin around its border an opportunity for a life-giving, chaos-breaking, transforming, creative conversation between you and the eternal God.

To have a conversation in the blank spaces holds a particular challenge. You must be comfortable with the wide-open space—not just of the margin on the page but also of the invitation to sit still

TO LIVE
sacred-
LIVES...

pick up !!
a pen !

for an extended period of time, thereby creating the space for a real conversation.

Or maybe you do not need to be comfortable with the blank spaces. Maybe you just need to be willing to become comfortable with the stillness. Or you need to be willing to brave the discomfort; I keep finding that some of the most fruitful spiritual experiences of my life come when I am willing to brave the discomfort.

God's best work occurs in the margins. If we have the courage to step into that wide-open space, God will meet us there.

Sacred Edges

Perhaps, like me, you have hoped to connect to God by reading straight through the Bible from Genesis to Revelation—every chapter, every verse, every levitical law and psalm, every parable and proverb. With great resolve, you have laid out a chart and set to reading. Genesis unfolds in its praise of creation and prose of family life. We are drawn into the joy of childbirth, the drama of jealousy, and the crazy grace of providence. In Exodus, we are amazed by the salvation story of slaves escaping from Egypt led by the everyman Moses. Even the building of the tabernacle, as detailed as the story gets, creates awe and wonder as a place for worship is dedicated and great offerings of each person's skill and craft and resources culminate in its beautiful design. This is the dwelling place of God, and at this point in our journey to connect with God, we are completely connected and even awed.

And then we get to the book of Leviticus.

Have you done this? Made it through Genesis and Exodus, then turned the page to Leviticus and those burnt offerings and lists of laws and been completely done. All resolve goes up in ashes with those pigeons and turtledoves. So much for the chart and the good intentions. When the daily discipline of Bible reading is already slighted by the sleepy eyes for the evening devotion, or the ruse of busy days for the morning reading, and then those Leviticus chapters unfold, we can't help but get interrupted. In my head, I know that Leviticus is the story of how God met God's people, of how Israel engaged with and danced with and lived with the living God. But sometimes my eyes glaze over, nonetheless.

This is precisely where the margins matter. The very place in scripture where we so often *stop* reading is precisely the place we need to deeply listen. God cares about the margins, and that message resounds in Leviticus 23:22: "When you harvest your land's produce, you must not harvest all the way to the edge of your field; and don't gather every remaining bit of your harvest. Leave these items for the poor and the immigrant; I am the LORD your God."

Here, God says very clearly, the edges matter.

God is referring to the fields for the harvest, but this same principle matters for the margins of our Bibles as well. For the fields, setting aside the edge created a sacred space, an offering of sorts, for the poor and the widowed, the migrant and the immigrant, to glean and gather a portion of the harvest for their nourishment.

When I read these words, I can't help but wonder about the connections and conversations that occurred around those edges as strangers met, shared in the bounty, exchanged words of wisdom, offered encouragement for the journey. This edge became a place of new connections, an intersection wherein those who might not cross paths in daily life made acquaintance and found strength from one another.

Is it possible that our Bibles are just like these fields? Perhaps this might seem contradictory at first. If God says save the edges, then why would we go and fill the margins of our Bibles?

But I wonder if there is an invitation in this text from Leviticus for us to think about how we look at the margins of our Bibles. Could this border be a sacred edge? A place for offering? A place for firstfruits? A place to invite in the outside world we might otherwise keep at bay? A place to engage in new conversations with the

WHEN YOU HARVEST YOUR LAND'S PRODUCE, YOU MUST NOT HARVEST ALL THE WAY TO THE EDGE OF YOUR FIELD; & DON'T GATHER EVERY REMAINING BIT OF YOUR HARVEST. Leave these items for the poor & the immigrant; I AM THE LORD YOUR GOD. CEB, Leviticus 23:22

fields of harvest

poor, the widowed, the migrant, the orphaned child? Perhaps those conversations are sometimes with a stranger we hear about in the comings and goings of our daily life and then bring to God in prayer on the page. Or perhaps those conversations are with whatever part of ourselves is poor, widowed, a stranger in a new land, an orphaned child who has lost something precious. What if the Bible were our first field? A place to practice this discipline—of making sacred the edge—that we then take and practice in the other portions and fields of our lives?

Ironically, maybe, it is precisely in Leviticus that we learn how important connecting with God on the pages of our Bibles really is. The list of instructions in the text of Leviticus could be read as ho-hum and humdrum, or they can be seen as a lifeline—a whispered secret to living. Leviticus 23 is all about the spiritual discipline of margins—that is, keeping the edges of our fields, our days, our weeks, our hearts, our minds, our lives open and available to the surprising work of God.

Wouldn't it be amazing to see what could happen if we could keep such a practice? My hope and prayer, in the pages of this particular book, is that praying in the edges of our Bibles becomes a witness and a way into keeping those margins open in other parts of our lives. Then, in that sacred edge, new crops might be cultivated.

Wide-Open Spaces

Writing in the margins is about cultivation—finding that blank space that frames all of life, and creating an atmosphere inside that precious one-inch rim of breathing room. Writing in the margins is about finding a new way in the midst of confusion. It is the back and forth that comes from spending time with an old friend who knows you better than you know yourself.

Writing in the margins is about making sacred connections between ancient text and present day—an arc spanning time and space—that intersects the now and the real and the sometimes overwhelming, and finds wisdom and depth from those connections.

Writing in the margins is about bridging the distance from word to world and finding a new horizon as those two connect. Writing in the margins is a way of finding spaciousness—a spacious yes, a gracious no, and a ripe and pregnant maybe for the varying conversations and decisions of your life.

It's creating a space, having a conversation, making connections, and venturing forth from that place to a holy and changed life—transformed.

Mostly, writing in the margins is an offering—an act of making sacred the borders of our days and the edges of our prayer—as we connect and converse in new ways at this sacred intersection.

In this book you will find an invitation to cultivate, converse, connect, and change as you engage the breadth around the page by connecting the depth of scripture to the depth of your soulful experience in living.

This is a place to doodle, a place to write with your nondominant hand, a place to scribble, a place to pray, a place to write things that surprise you, a place to be honest. It is a place to think hard but not to overthink. It is a place to pray your heart out, but not piously. It is a place for you alone—in conversation with God.

In an article on marginalia in *The New York Times*, Dirk Johnson captures just what kind of conversation writing in the margins can be:

> *Studs Terkel, the oral historian, was known to admonish friends who would read his books but leave them free of markings. He told them that reading a book should not be a passive exercise, but rather a raucous conversation.*

"...Reading a book should not be a passive exercise, but rather a RAUCOUS CONVERSATION"...

— STUDS TERKEL

Writing in the margins of your Bible is, simply, a way of having an ongoing, raucous conversation with God.

Growing up in south Louisiana, my dad and I would venture to the local public library on Saturday afternoons and check out stacks of books. There were no better days than these. We would get home and collapse on the sofa with the piles beside us, and more days than not, listen to the afternoon thunderstorm roll through. I remember sitting with those books knowing that the border around the edges kept the world at bay. The margins created a sacred space where a whole new world could be explored.

Now, as an adult, I crave that time when the world stopped and all that existed was the comfort of my dad and the space those margins checked out from the library created. All was well with the world, for a moment, those afternoons. Sometimes I find that peace again when I work in the edges of my Bible. That wide-open space, that work in the edge of the margins, creates wide-open spaces for me to breathe, but even more to serve as I reach out to others in justice, humility, and mercy having been strengthened by my time in the margins.

In this book, we'll learn about all sorts of margin-writers who had raucous conversations in their margins: musicians from Elvis to Bach, writers from Melville to Mary Karr, artists and doodlers, sinners and saints. We'll learn from ordinary folks like you and me who unearthed lives of meaning in the depths of their margins. And we'll learn how margins recovered the lost language of the Wampanoag Indians. We'll learn how the margins nurtured someone's love. And we'll see how the margins of a young girl, McKenzie, led to the building of orphanages halfway around the world.

Our invitation to write, and in so doing to set things right, comes from our creator God—the one who writes creation into existence. Because we have a God who writes, we have an invitation to write. And, because we have a God who sets things right, we might just be made right in our practice of writing.

Virginia Woolf says, "The beauty of the world . . . has two edges, one of laughter, one of anguish." I wonder if our Bibles meet those two edges of laughter and anguish every time we open the pages.

In my life, I've known a lot of laughter, and just a bit of anguish. In my ministry, I've seen both through and through. I go to the margins to remember the laughter and lament the anguish. These are the sacred edges of our world, our lives, and of this amazing text.

We meet this sacred edge with the Bible in one hand and a pen in the other.

* 2 edges

LAUGHTER | anguish

Connecting with God

Renee Aukeman Prymus

It has been a long time since I have picked up a Bible to read it, and when I do, it's a newer Bible without a lot of marginalia.

Today I picked up my duct-taped Bible and riffled through it. When I got this small, hand-sized Bible, at age fifteen, it had a maroon hardcover on it. Inside the front cover was a sticker with the approximate years of various ages and which Bible characters likely lived when. The Bible was with me on a hiking trip through Israel for two weeks when I was a teenager.

I carried this Bible everywhere between the ages of fifteen and twenty-one. At some point in college, the maroon cover fell off and I reupholstered the Bible with duct tape, taking care to create a tab for a pen and a pocket for my index cards at the back of the Bible. Since the Bible was so well used, the pages should be frail and pliable, but the Bible fell in the pool one summer while I was lifeguarding at a Christian camp, and the pages were never the same after that. All my purple-ink marginalia has faded to bright pink.

I flip through the pages of this Bible, and it's similar to walking through the pages of my journals. Matthew contains big scrawls of my high school handwriting in Israel about the spice trade helping to fund Jesus' ministry. Smudges from flowers cover the pages of 2 Kings 16:9–17:41, where I've now tucked encouraging quotes from former students, rewritten Psalms, and notes from sermons. Colossians and 1 Corinthians, both books that helped me through college, are filled with underlining.

When I look at these notes, at my very early, very evident devotion to God, my mind flips through pages of thoughts.

First, a twinge of guilt. Where did my avid Bible-reading days go? As I look through those pages, I stand in awe at my younger self. I was dedicated, devoted, and diligent in my studies, my prayers, and my relationship with God. I know that person is still inside me, still dedicated and devoted. Maybe I can discover her again.

Next to Exodus 14:13-14, where Moses tells the people not to be afraid in the face of the Egyptians, I wrote "prescription for unexpected life." Somehow, moving back into the margins might help me live into that adventure.

On the Pages of Your Bible

- Open your Bible to Psalm 1 and read this prayer, which asks that we might become rooted in the word of God, just like "a tree replanted by streams of water, which bears fruit at just the right time" (Psalm 1:3). Around the margins of this page, muse about the fruits that might come from planting yourself ever more deeply in the Scriptures—how do you hope your commitment to engage God's word on the pages of your Bible bring will bring growth to your life?

- Take several deep breaths. As you breathe in, think the words "wide open," and as you breathe out, think the word "space." As you breathe in and out this breath prayer, allow God to create wide-open space within you. Simply look at the margins of your Bible to see that wide-open space and imagine what possibilities God might have for you there.

- Just as we often want our margins "justified" against the right edge of the page, we look to God for justification. Through the work of Christ, God makes things "right" in our lives and invites us to live holy lives. Galatians 2:16 is a key verse in the Bible that proclaims that truth. Turn to Galatians, and read 2:11-21. Take notes in the margin in three ways. First, write down the words, images, or line that stands out to you in bold. Second, write down any questions you have. Third, choose one phrase from the passage that you especially want to hold onto and paraphrase it—write it down in your own words.

- What if your Bible was a field? Consider it a crop waiting to be harvested. Open the Bible and look at the layout of the land. Then, linger on the invitation of Leviticus 23. What might grow and be cultivated in this sacred edge? What might be offered? What crop is growing there now? What do you hope will be collected in the next harvest?

- Virginia Woolf speaks to anguish and laughter as the two edges of life. Read any of the following texts and reflect in the margins on the relationship between joy and pain in God's world:

Isaiah 61:1-6   Psalm 30
Ecclesiastes 3:1-8   Matthew 5:1-12

LOVE LETTERS

I contend, quite bluntly,
that marking up a book
is not an act of mutilation but of love.

—Mortimer Adler

Writing in the margins caused quite a scandal in Scotland.

At the Gallery of Modern Art in Glasgow two artists in residence, Anthony Schrag and David Malone, invited gallery-goers to scribble in the scriptures. The invitation was made in particular to anyone who felt excluded from the Bible and resulted in marginalia unprintable here. The *Times of London* criticized the exhibit as desecration.

The difference between writing into the Bible at the museum and writing into the margins of your own Bible is important. Margin writing is devotion, not exhibition. Margin writing is consecration, not desecration.

Andrea Minichiello Williams responded to the exhibit by saying,

* devotion & consecration (not exhibition = or desecration)

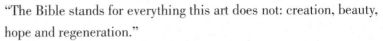

"The Bible stands for everything this art does not: creation, beauty, hope and regeneration."

For us, the question is this: Is marginalia desecration or a sacred conversation? Is writing in the margins an act of graffiti, or an offering of gratitude?

William Mwizerwa, director of the Legacy Mission Village for African refugees in Nashville, Tennessee, is a survivor from Rwanda. He shares that struggle:

> When I was little we did not have many Bibles in my country for many reasons. During my young age Bibles were printed out of the country and distributed on a little number. One Bible was used by a big group. That means we didn't have individual Bibles as kids. Everyone had a great respect for the Bible, so taking notes in the margin was going to be a problem. Instead of writing in the Bible they encouraged people to memorize verses. I got my individual Bible in high school. It was mandatory. And my parents did not let me write in it because I was supposed to pass it to my brother. But today the new generation writes in the margins, which looks like a kind of disrespect to the Bible for the old people.

For William, margin writing goes against everything he has been taught about the Bible. The Bible is precious, for a whole community and not just for an individual person.

Nudging ourselves into the margins, to mark up a sacred text, can feel disrespectful.

But there is another way to think of scribbling: the scribbles are, perhaps, an act of deep internalization. Perhaps it is exactly these scribbles that lead to creation, beauty, hope, and even resurrection. Maybe these scribbles are less lawless desecration, and much more an act of consecration.

Marking the biblical text is something like beginning a love letter. As Mortimer Adler says, *I contend, quite bluntly, that marking up a book is not an act of mutilation but of love.*

THE QUESTION
- desecration or sacred conversation?
- graffiti or offering of gratitude?

Cryptic Letters

My friend Chris tells the story of her father's Bible. One day, flipping through the Bible, a family member looked into the margins of her father's Bible and found cryptic letters and dates:

Isaiah 12

August 11, 1946

"ILE"

Isaiah 13

August 14, 1946

"ILMW"

Isaiah 14

August 20, 1946

"ISLE"

Not your usual acronym. The first date was June 9, 1946, their wedding day.

Finally, someone realized:

I love Elaine.	*ILE*
I love my wife.	*ILMW*
I still love Elaine.	*ISLE*

As they looked through scripture, they found more acronyms and additional dates:

February 14, 1950, February 14, 1951 . . . through the turn of the century, February 14, 1999, and into the twenty-first century.

Sixty-six years of wedding anniversaries marked by these letters.

"I love my wife." This was the acronym her father wrote into his Bible on his wedding night, and every year since.

YEARS AGO, a colleague in writing, Rachel Coyne Vater shared her incredible margin story:

Our Bibles were very special to us growing up. We never placed any other books or objects on top of them in our home. In the front of my father's Bible, he recorded for each of his four daughters our names, our dates of salvation, and our dates of baptism. He taught us how to sit attentively in church and take notes, and we would discuss the sermon in the half hour car ride home. Very special passages of the Bible would be underlined in a pen if we felt they were especially meaningful to us. My father even had a special silver pen he would use to make careful notes in his. I was less easy about jotting anything into the margins of my Bible. I wasn't sure if it was okay or not to mark up my Bible with my childish handwriting. But one day, as my father and I were sitting side-by-side in church, he leaned over and wrote "daddy" in the margin of my Bible. I smiled up at him, and carefully wrote "Rachel" in my little girl handwriting in the margin of his. "Now every time we see that, you'll think of me, and I'll think of you," he whispered quietly in my ear. And he was right. Sometimes we would see it in church together, and we would silently point at it and share a smile.

The family jokes, knowing the practical nature of the father and grandfather, that he must have written on his wedding day, "I lost my wallet" as an acronym in panic.

But now, fifty years later, some are marked: ISLMW. I still love my wife.

When the family first discovered the letters in the margins, the family was disturbed that the father had been writing in the margins on his wedding night. Did he not have other things to attend to?

But it was in the margins of scripture that the family learned about his act of consecration. These letters and dates, scribbled in love, were the beginning of a great love affair that was founded in the love of God.

Framed in our house, I have our daughters' earliest love letters. Those "I love you moms" scribbled with hearts and flowers. These expressions endure as a particular witness to an irreplaceable time and place: childhood. Is that not true of every age as well? That each moment, taken note of, calls for celebration and remembrance?

Recently a college student I know was reading *The Shack*. After reading it once for self-understanding, the student read the story again while praying for his girlfriend. As he prayed for her place of struggle with God and her areas of grief and loss, he wrote in the margins of the page the prayers he named for her and their life together.

When he passed on the book for her reading, at first she did not get it. The writing on the sidelines was a distraction, not a help. And then, as the story unfolded, she realized the depth of his love for her. The prayers were love letters named in the margins. In the margins, a conversation began about God, faith, suffering, and ultimate hope. The two texts, complementary of each other, the words to *The Shack*, and the markings of her boyfriend, created a deep story of love in her life.

Marking up a book is not an act of mutilation. Marking a book can be an act of love.

★ EACH MOMENT, taken note of, calls for CELEBRATION & REMEMBRANCE (TRUE!)

Marking a Book

Mortimer Adler says there are three kinds of book owners.

The first has the fancy books—pages neat and binding unbent. These books sit untouched. Adler argues these can't even be "books" if they have not been read, they are simply "wood pulp and ink."

The second type of book owner has all the fancy books, most unread, but within that collection there are a few that have been read through. But most, sit shiny and new. Unused. Unloved. Unread.

The third type of book owner has scribbled in the margins, marked on the front and back covers, turned many a dog-eared page and a few of the books in the collection might even be considered downright worn out. This is the person who owns books. This is the person who is willing to fall in love.

I think we can say specifically for the Bible what Adler says about books in general. The cultivation of a conversation in the margins of scripture is one step toward falling in love with, or deepening one's love for, God.

Perhaps, polemically, we could flirt with the idea that an unmarked book, an unmarked Bible, is an unloved book.

Falling in love requires dates, important get-to-know-each-other times. Falling in love depends on conversation, important get-to-know-each-other times. And falling in love necessitates risk, that important leap of faith, where in honesty a person puts himself or herself out there to be met halfway by the other.

Isn't that what time with God in the margins looks like?

This is conversation, not desecration. This is consecration, all because of those important dates scrawled into the margin, where with time and devotion the reader and the writer have fallen in love all over again. The margins offer a place to fall in love, again and again and again.

Falling in Love

Susan has Jackie Bush to thank for falling in love.

Forty years since that fourth-grade Sunday school class, Susan is still writing in the margins of her Bible after Mrs. Bush not only permitted the class to write in their Sunday school Bibles but also *encouraged* them to do so. Now, decades later, Susan provided her own children with wide-margined Bibles, pens, and permission. What if Mrs. Bush had said no?

Insights might have been missed. Memories disappeared. Favorite passages forgotten. Genealogical histories vanished. Questions lost. Nuances neglected.

Jackie Bush taught decades of kids how to fall in love—with the pages of their Bible, with the God who came alive in the story, with the neighbor to their left and to their right, even with their own scuffy-shoed, bedraggled selves.

I wonder if the love letters that emerge in the margins are letters written to God, self, and neighbor. The margins of my Bible are a place that I can learn to live out the two greatest commands—to love God with heart, mind, and soul and to love our neighbor as ourself. Loving God, self, and neighbor can all unfold in the margins of the page.

Within these love stories there are always those two edges: laughter and anguish. Thank God the margins help us sort out both of those dimensions of our lives.

Loving God

Dr. H. A. Ironside, the long-tenured pastor of Moody Memorial Church outside of Chicago, wrote in the cracks of his Bible. The words tucked against the spine reflect the spirit of a man who began his ministry as a street preacher, pounding the cracks of the pavement looking for the soul that was lost. In Ironside's Bible are drawings of the cross, prayers written by others, the sketch of a hand pierced by a nail, exegetical insights, mnemonic devices, and tools for teaching and preaching. Throughout the Bible is a scattering of Chinese characters revealing Ironside's interest in learning the Chinese language. The cracks of his Bible reveal his prayers for strength in his life journey. He quotes the "testimony of a ruined business man" who prayed, *"When I was rich, I had God in everything; now I am poor and I have everything in God."*

Ruminations about his love for God, the sense of "everything" he finds in God, are in Ironside's margins. Tucked far into the crease of his Bible is the motto of Francis of Assisi, *Deus Meus, Mea Omnia.* The words are powerful in their simplicity and timelessness: *My God and My all.*

Loving Self

Several summers ago, I journeyed with my mom and daughter Leah to my mother's homeland in Helsinki, Finland. The journey came after a tough period in ministry. On my birthday, a Sunday, we made a special visit to a fascinating church: The Michael Agricola Lutheran Church. Every Sunday night at seven, the church offers a worship service called "The Thomas Mass." Its mission is to bring the doubters in. I couldn't get there fast enough. I doubted everything about myself, my ministry, my sense of call. That deep sense of self-doubt is anything but love.

The website for the Michael Agricola Lutheran Church encourages, "The St. Thomas Mass invites doubters and seekers to celebrate, worship God, serve their neighbor and grow together." And then continues, "Those who feel sinful and weak in faith are especially welcome."

In an incredible act of hospitality, a Finnish man named Mati translates every worship service into English. All of us were able to hear the worship service whispered directly into our ears. Worship was wonderful.

Near the end of the service, Mati translated the prayer that led us into communion. I felt like it was written just for me that night:

> *Prayer helps you listen to yourself and to God*
> *who speaks in silence in the noise of everyday.*
> *This quiet moment will give you rest. . . .*
> *Let God love you.*

Let God love you. The deepest prayer of my heart found hope with these four words. I wrote them in my Bible next to the text that was preached in worship that night: John 7:37-38: "All who are thirsty should come to me! All who believe in me should drink!"

With this encouragement, with newfound love for self, I was now ready to return home to offer a few love letters to others to do just the same: Love God, Love Self, Love Neighbor.

Loving Neighbor

My friend John speaks of the back and forth between the margins of his Bible and the people on the edges of his day.

> *My margins get me thinking of people in the margins of my life. The people who are in the periphery of my life story. These are the people I may see on my way to school, on the bus, or even people at school or in my church. These are the people on the side of the road in the Good Samaritan story. These people are in my margins because they add to the main text of my daily life. Although I may never speak to them, they can alter my mood or my day, teach me in their actions, or cause me to raise questions of society. Sometimes I*

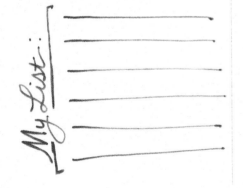

WHO ARE THE PEOPLE in the PERIPHARY - margins - OF MY LIFE STORY? Who am i called to be a Neighbor to?

My List:

wonder if praying in the margins is what really helps to nurture in me God's call to love our neighbor.

In the margins of our Bibles is space that can help us see the neighbors we might otherwise move to the margins of our lives.

Jackie Bush, H. A. Ironside, John Magnuson, and yes even I have learned to love through writing in our Bibles. Here, we are pushed to the edges of the page to pray and to fall in love. Here, we write love letters—to God, to ourselves, and to the person otherwise on the margin of our day. We learn to fall in love. And then, we're poised and ready to love, again and again and again. Marking the page is not an act of mutilation. Marking the page is an act of love.

Connecting with God

Nicole Hunter and Nathan Hunter

It was November 26, 2011, when we received our first large-margined Bible: a cozy abode of our very own to accumulate thoughts, ah-ha moments, discoveries, relations, and revelations . . . important ones. A visiting place where we will discover, prosper, reveal, and grow as individuals . . . together. We've both had one before; only that one was dwelled upon with a single set of eyes. Now we have one on which to collaborate.

We need large margins now because there are two of us operating it. We haven't jotted any thoughts in it yet. We will in years to come, as we get married this year and throughout our marriage in the years to come. Inside the cover, stationed on the right side of the page, written in familiar, delicate handwriting, are holy words from one of our role models.

Among the words was the sentence, "We look forward to seeing how God works in your life together . . . a life full of love, joy, peace, and faith."

Fast-forwarding to the future, we look forward to giving our children a large-margined Bible, for it is the complete representation of what we're supposed to use this ancient work to do: take notes to best learn to love, spread joy, and extend peace throughout the earth, all while living in the faith of God.

On the Pages of Your Bible

- This chapter shares a few love stories. Turn to 1 Corinthians 13, the great text on love in the New Testament. Write in the margins key concepts gleaned from this passage.

- Psalm 86:12 echoes the affirmation of Francis of Assisi, *Deus Meus, Mea Omnia (My God and My All)*. In the margin next to Psalm 86:12, or anywhere else that seems apt, write Assisi's cry.

- Read Matthew 22:39 and consider the delicate balance between love for neighbor and love for self. How do you maintain the balance? What are your checks and balances for keeping the two in tandem? Write a note in the margin to remind yourself.

- Next, read Luke 10:25-37 and write in the margin your reflections on the ways God instructs us to love our neighbors.

- Jackie Bush has taught hundreds of children through the years to fall in love with God on the pages of their Bibles. Read Deuteronomy 11:19. In the margin, make a pledge to God for the way you might teach a child in your life about scripture.

FACING THE MARGINS
OF OUR LIVES

All experience is an arch wherethrough gleams
that untravelled world whose margin
fades for ever and for ever when I move.

—Alfred Lord Tennyson

Recently, Rich, a friend of mine and a margin-writer, passed away at age forty-nine of brain cancer. And though the words in his margins did not save his life, I wholeheartedly believe they saved him: they enlivened his spiritual life, and, I believe, made his illness more bearable.

In addition to being Rich's friend, I was his pastor, and the day after his death, his family entrusted me with his personal Bible; they asked that I use it as I prepared for Rich's funeral service. When they tucked into my hands his Bible, I had no idea the treasure that was in store. As I flipped through the pages, I was stunned, inspired, and challenged by its margins. There was laughter. There was anguish. There was a lotta love.

I have always been a margin-writer, but my notes are sporadic. In Rich's Bible I could see an intricate web of words: the prayers of his heart, the struggles of his mind, and the hopes for his soul, all penciled into the margins of scripture during the hardest course of his life. I could look at those notes and see a visual record of his days, and of his life with God.

As I turned through the pages, I read the reflections of a complicated and faithful man. Clear confessions are written in capital letters. Names of his daughters alight each page. State parks and country roads are named as Rich documented daily runs. The quality of light and quantity of deer are noted. Conversations with friends continue to unfold on the page. Thanksgivings unfold and erupt into exclamation marks. There are prayers for both yielding as well as holding strong. Discernment for his leadership in his workplace is expressed as well as prayers for developing leadership in others.

Rich's Bible is a living field. His marginalia evoke the secrets that God whispered daily into his hopeful ear and longing heart. And, Rich's Bible is a complex harvest of the comings and goings, the aching and failings, the longings and loving of his days. Rich wove meaning into his life through that one-inch space hugging the sides of the biblical text. The meaning and direction he found there, gave purpose and heart to each dimension of his life.

I see patterns of meaning inscripted into the pages of Rich's Bible. Looking back on his life, I see how those inscriptions posited positive change for himself, his family, and for others.

Rich's Bible reminds me that one reason I write in the margins of my Bible is this: I write so that I might find patterns of meaning. I write so that I might discover the Bible's patterns, and so that I might see more clearly how to pattern my own life thus.

PATTERNS of
MEANING

I'm Calling to You

On my desk, I keep a copy from page 999 of Rich's Bible. At the center of the page is Psalm 86. Originally a Psalm of David, it became the prayer of Rich. In the margins of the 8½-by-11-inch-page is the harvest of his days: dates, names, question marks, exclamation points, affirmations, questions, confessions, locations, places, and pleas cover the page. The prayer engages every word of the text. Words are circled, phrases underlined, arrows and lines connect everything. The lines and fragments on the page intertwined with the scriptural text become an intimate and intricate web of support. Scripture is a living text—intersecting all of life with words of prayer.

At the center of Rich's life was his family, church, and God. Yet the conversation Rich had with God was decidedly complex. Rich was in the habit of talking to God on his morning run while training for a marathon. In the midst of that training, Rich was diagnosed with a brain tumor. But his conversations with God continued, often in writing: it included prayers of thanksgiving and hopes for the future. On bad days, it became lament.

Those conversations with God—I think of them, simply, as "God talk"—found its way into the corners, margins, and edges of Rich's Bible. Connecting word and world, Rich talked with God about his life and mapped out his prayers and hopes for the days at hand.

I've always wondered what a glimpse into someone else's prayer life might look like. This printed page holds an insight into one man's life of prayer. The notes in the margin are organic and alive. Some were written in his very last days of life. Phrases like "You have Lord" and "He lives in me" and "I have been richly blessed" affirm Rich's deep belief. Prayers of unbelief cry out in words like "Transform me" and "I am calling to you."

I have been richly blessed!!

Praying in the Margins

Remember that image from Leviticus—the invitation to invite the poor and the widowed, the orphaned and the immigrant into the edges of your fields and offer the border as a prayer that their needs will be nourished? I can't help but see those incredible intersections on the sacred edge of Rich's Bible.

- Names are everywhere in Rich's margins. Here, he scrawled around the edges the names of coworkers, doctors, folks he met in the hospital, his kids, his neighbors. These names reflected people who shined with the light of Christ, or for whom darkness necessitated the prayers.

- Rich ran marathons and triathlons. Notations are made throughout his Bible when he read a scripture passage before or after training. He took notes on the weather, the date, the running partner, the degree of difficulty in his training, and most of all, where he saw God on his run that day.

- Lists are given throughout Rich's Bible listing moments along the journey of any given day, season, struggle, faith development, and year.

- Early in his life, writing in the margins helped him with the task of *discernment*: who he was, and what good work God was calling him to do in the world. What kind of father was God helping him to become, and what kind of husband, and what kind of son? All of those questions were sorted out, in part, on the margins of his Bible.

- As Rich read the Bible, I believe he heard songs echoing in his head from worship. Certain texts would call forth lines from hymns, "Our God Is an Awesome God," "Open the Eyes of My Heart, Lord," "Amazing Grace," and "It's All about You, Jesus" are just a few of the examples.

- Petitions for help fill the margins of Rich's New International Version. He wrote the simple word "help" over and over again.

Perhaps he used "help" as an acronym for: Heavy sigh, Engage the cry, Let it be said, Plead for what you need.

- Prayers for his children are etched in the edges. The names of his daughters, the needs he noticed they had, notations about moments with them are vivid on the pages.

- Sometimes the prayers are as simple as naming attributes of God or adjectives to describe God. Simple words like "awesome" and "holy" speak volumes of theology.

- Some pages of Rich's Bible almost resemble a road map, or a guide to his day. Whether it is locations, dates, buildings, parks, roadways, or running paths—lines, arrows, calendar dates, and place names create a visual map on many a page.

- A consistent ritual for Rich was making note of the rich blessings of the day. Whether it was the angle of the sun's light, the new growth on a tree, the beauty of his daughters, or a moment with his wife—all were blessings and thanksgivings named before God.

From Rich's Bible, I learned to face the edges. Facing the edge—pushing up against the things in life that separate me from other people and to encounter those parts of myself I find scary—is something I don't always like to do. Facing the edge is acknowledging whatever conflict, doubt, frustration, or anxiety that ate at my day and then naming it in a realized prayer, not a pushed-aside hassle. Facing the edge is gleaning the good while placing the not-so-good into God's hands.

I Believe; Help My Unbelief!

Amid all the many prayers Rich prayed in his margins, two stand out to me. First are the prayers Rich prayed near the end of his life that turned on the theme of belief and disbelief. Later in life,

FACING the EDGE

* gleaning the good while placing the "NOT SO GOOD" into God's hands

marginal writing became Rich's lifeline. That line of ink held him together in a way that the tubing of the hospital wires and feeds could not. The act of articulation, naming in honesty the prayers of his life before God, was an act of faith. That leap into the unknown was grounded in belief, but propelled by disbelief. The belief and the unbelief, the faith and the stunned shock of illness, made for a rich, sometimes painful conversation with God. At the edge of those margins, conversation about the deepest pulse of life emerged.

"I believe; help my unbelief" (NRSV). The Common English Bible offers an even clearer statement, "I have faith; help my lack of faith!" (Mark 9:24). This may be the most honest and restrained prayer in the Bible. Its simplicity belies the complexity behind these five words. At our best, here are our two hands clasped in prayer: one pressing on the other in belief. The other pressing hard against faith in disbelief. At our worst, here are our two arms flailing in prayer: in rage, anguish, grief, or desperately lashing out.

" I have FAITH; help my lack of faith ! "
- MARK 9:24
CEB

Perhaps the margins of our Bibles offer a space for just such an honest prayer. A prayer grounded in the text, the very Word of Jesus Christ, but also a prayer propelled by our own struggles and disbelief as we engage in conversation with the world around us. This honesty is what the margins require and allow.

On the pages of Rich's Bible, he wrote words of belief, such as "It is all about you Jesus," and "God, you are cool!" and "I have humble adoration." But he also wrote about his unbelief: "I need trust," and "Help me, Lord." On the pages of my own Bible, I have written similar prayers in my margins as well.

This is where we all need to be encouraged. Be honest. Write your life into the margins. In gratitude, name what you "get" for a moment about who this Jesus is. In hope, be honest about your shortcomings, your questions, your deepest sighs. This is the place to pray nonstop. To put those prayers on paper. To move them from gut to God.

Pray without Ceasing

In addition to Rich's ruminations about belief and unbelief, I am struck, when I look at page 999, by the ceaselessness of his prayers.

First Thessalonians 5:17 invites people of faith to "pray without ceasing" (NRSV). I have always wondered what, precisely, this means—it cannot, surely, mean saying the Lord's Prayer over and over again. It can't mean doing *lectio divina* around the clock. It can't even mean making marginal notes in your Bible all the time.

Rich's Bible began to teach me the meaning of the instructions to the Thessalonians. The act of putting pen to paper, in the margins of the Bible, allows for that continual prayer while scripture is engaged. In the margin, the text moves into our lives and we nudge our lives into the text. In other words, Rich did not write in his Bible twenty-four hours a day—but the writing he did do allowed the Scriptures to take root in his soul and mind, such that he was in them, and in prayer, ceaselessly.

Praying without ceasing requires creativity. Constant prayer is not easy. Think of the many things each day that might distract you from praying. Constancy necessitates creativity. Rich's Bible bursts with that creative, constant prayer—the cry of his heart emerges on every page there.

In my margin next to 1 Thessalonians 5:17 I have written these three words: *cry, creativity,* and *constancy*. Prayer is crying out. How are you crying out to God in your margins? Prayer that never goes "without" has to be creative. How are you being creative in your margin-making prayers? And prayer that is ceaseless is of course, constant. What are you learning about God's constant presence to you through your practice of margin writing?

True Surrender

As I write this now, I still cannot believe that cancer claimed the life of Rich who left behind his wife and three daughters. But I know that Rich experienced regenerated life through his authentic and unafraid conversation with God in the margins of his Bible. In the margin, Rich found a relationship deeper than lines read in a text. In the margins, despair rearranged itself into a God who was praised. In the margin, Rich sometimes prayed for a specific out-come—healing—but he ultimately focused on the incoming grace of God.

Near the end of his life, he wrote the word "CANCER" in bold letters. And he wrote "True surrender," in a barely visible hand, on the bottom of the same page. This was a powerful negotiation—a prayer for healing, and a prayer of release and acceptance. Both prayers were true and heartfelt. And the margins of Rich's Bible were wide enough to hold them both. Could it be that between the page and the pen, Rich found the capacity to surrender not in a way that negated his life, but in a way that validated every aspect of his life?

I keep a page of Rich's Bible at hand because it reminds me how I might find in the margins a way to pray without ceasing. It invites me to negotiate the fragile ground between belief and unbelief over a lifetime. And it invites me to hold before God my pleas for help, change, and healing, and also to hold before God my surrender to God's arms.

Rich did not intend to write a love letter, but he did. His margins inspire mine. For each of us leaning into belief, learning to pray without ceasing, and living into a true surrender is a lifelong task. We take notes of our learning in the margins.

[TRUE
SURRENDER]

Connecting with God

Diane Glancy

I have many Bibles, starting with a childhood Bible given to me at confirmation in the Methodist Church, probably in 1948 when I was seven. I have older Bibles that belonged to my grandmother, my mother, my aunt, and an uncle.

In 1971, I bought a Scofield Bible with a Moroccan leather cover. It is the one I used when I went to Grace and Glory Bible School, and attended the Grace and Glory Tabernacle. It was what I would call a thorough church. The pages of my Bible from those years are lined with notes. They are written in the margins, upside down on the bottom of the page, and crosswise across the top. Some of the handwriting has bled and is hard to read. Many of the pages are loose. But the notes stick with me.

Beside Psalm 102, for instance, I had written, "Jesus' feelings on earth." A rejection psalm. Jesus was a heavenly being out of his natural place. Beside verse 6 (I am like a pelican of the wilderness; I am like an owl of the desert [NRSV]), I had written, "a root out of dry ground."

This is the way I felt recently crossing the desert on a move from Kansas to California. The local movers I decided to use had gotten lost. Their truck had broken down. A two-day trip was now four. My car is old. It was 105 degrees. I was at a low point. I stopped at a rest area on I-40 east of Barstow, California, and laid my head on a pillow for a moment. I was an owl in the desert. But Christ had gone before me. I felt the root. The spark that held me. I could drive on.

On the Pages of Your Bible

- "Pray without ceasing" is an invitation from 1 Thessalonians 5:17. Turn to 1 Thessalonians 5:17 and let your pen glide across the page in continual prayer. After you have finished writing the words, take a deep breath, and read your words aloud as prayer.

- Mark 9:24 names an incredible prayer, "I have faith; help my lack of faith!" (Mark 9:24). On the left side of your margin, write down the areas in your life where you have faith. On the right side of your margin, write down the areas in your life where you lack faith. To bridge the distance between the two, write a prayer connecting the two across the top margin on the page.

- Rich wrote the simple words "True surrender" in his margin. James 4:7-10 is a prayer for surrender. Read this text. Then, write your paraphrase of the passage in the margin.

LAYING OUT THE GOLDEN RATIO OF PAGE DESIGN

Let your life lightly dance on the edge . . . like dew on the tip of a leaf.

—Rabindranath Tagore

A Look at the Edges

Open your Bible on a flat surface. Take a look at the text. Then, take a look at the edges.

Margins would not exist without content. A margin is formed around something that matters. The black print on the white page, amazingly, communicates the deepest truth about God. We scan the lines and suddenly curves and strokes, dots and dashes, straight lines and crooked create sacred text. The core of its message transcends space and time. What is received into our core grounds us in the here and now and gives us purpose and meaning.

Next, look at the layout of the pages. Book typesetters have a complex set of terminology to describe the orientation of the seemingly simple construction of the pages before you.

On your left is the "verso" page. On your right is the "recto" page. Down the center, along the open spine of the book, is the "gutter." Along the verso edge is the "left padding." Along the recto edge is the "right padding." The top and bottom of the page as well both have "padding" as their margin.

Since the publication of the Gutenberg Bible to the most recent presentation of *The Message,* the elements of page design and the elaborate system for determining the margins is a high and holy endeavor. For example, in the Gutenberg Bible a specific layout came to be described as the "golden ratio" for page construction. This layout was said to have "divine" proportions. The golden canon of page design is a secret to the layout of the text on the page. The height of the type area on the page is equal to the width of a single page. Through a complex graph of circles, squares, and triangles alongside the divine ratio of 2:3, the layout artist arrives at a page layout mysteriously harmonious to the unsuspecting reader.

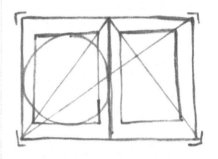

If we find divine proportions on the page, maybe we might find a mysteriously harmonious way of laying out our lives? If the "golden canon" can do such great things in page design, maybe it might help us live into the secrets of the golden rule?

While we might read the ratios of numbers giving expression to dimensions on the page and our heads start to spin, publishers see these ratios as the key to consumption. Robert Bringhurst, author of *Elements of Typographic Style,* offers this description:

> *The page is . . . a visible and tangible proportion, silently sounding the thoroughbass of the book. On it lies the textblock, which must answer to the page. The two together—page and textblock— produce an antiphonal geometry. That geometry alone can bond the reader to the book. Or conversely, it can put the reader to sleep, or put the reader's nerves on edge, or drive the reader away.*

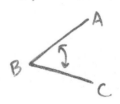

I need the margins. They give my life much-needed dimension. I need that circumscription of space to make a little sense of my life. But even more so, much more so, I need those words on the page. Burdens would remain way too heavy without the light and life of scripture. I really depend on those words whispered by Christ in the book of Matthew: "Come to me, all you who are struggling hard and carrying heavy loads, and I will give you rest. Put on my yoke, and learn from me. I'm gentle and humble. And you will find rest for yourselves. My yoke is easy to bear, and my burden is light" (Matthew 11:28-30).

On the page, I can lay out those burdens. But even more so, I can take on that yoke that is much easier to bear. Next to *yoke* in the margin of my Bible, I've written in the word *syzygy*. In Greek, it means "yoked together with." In English, it gets translated in a number of ways, depending on the discipline. In science, it means the pairing of cells. In poetry, it means the internal stress of sentence. I know something about both stress and the mishaps that can come in the pairing of cells. The reason I mention this great word here is not just for the Scrabble players of this world, but for the very incredible fact that *syzygy* is the only word in the English language that has three letter *y*s. Just like the word, life sometimes feels like it has way too many whys, too.

Sometimes I try and sort out those whys in the margins. The why of my daughter's Down Syndrome. The whys of motherhood and ministry. The why of purpose. The why of circumstance. The why of lament. The why of deepest grief. The why of Newtown, Connecticut. These whys fill our days and yet there are so few places to lay these burdens down.

In other words, the margins matter. The margins help us keep our interest. The margins bind us to the book so that its essence might be engaged, not tossed away.

So the margins serve several purposes:

- the space creates room for your left and right thumbs to grab hold of the book;
- the margin creates a frame, setting apart the artwork of typesetting;
- the margin offers breathing room; a mental space between word and world that sets the two apart;
- the margins cultivate a space where a certain conversation might happen; and
- there, in that sacred space, is an invitation for pen to beset against the page, for God talk.

In our laps, the margins are clear and tidy. Three-fourths of an inch on the left and right padding, two inches below, and one inch on top. The clarity provides room for creativity. The structure offers space.

But why is it in our lives those blank spaces are so much harder to find? And when we do find them, instead of breathing in that sacred space, why are we so much more likely to fill in that place?

Where Is Your Margin?

Do you have any margin in your life? Have you found that "golden canon," that "divine proportion" that creates the space you need to think, reflect, breathe, and act?

The margin that allows the space for you to be in the presence of God?

The margin where in silence the heart is stilled and prayers are named?

The margin being that structure of support creating a solid boundary?

A margin is an edge, a border, and a blank space that denotes the end of a space otherwise filled. A margin is an allowance, a measure, and a safety deposit. A margin is a place on the edge, a border between two realities. A margin is a place on the verge, a place full of possibility.

When our lives don't have a margin then we are pushed to the limit, overworked, exhausted, running on empty. A friend suggests that a huge problem of the twenty-first century is margin erosion.

The invitation to look toward the margin comes from a God who cares about the margins. The God who cares about sacred spaces, people's faces, and wide-open places. Deep breaths. Long conversations.

Writing in the margins is an opportunity to have a conversation with God. Like talking with an old friend over a cup of tea, this almighty God cares about you as an intimate friend.

No blank spaces.

No room to write.

No pages in my life not unfilled from edge to edge.

How do you prayerfully write in the margins when your life has none?

In a dream one night, while writing this book, I searched every corner of the house for a page unfilled—a place that had some small edge of white where there would be room to write.

But in the dream, not one single sheet contained any margin—everything was filled to the very edge.

Creating Space

The margins of my Bible work in a sort of loop: I need to clear out a little space in my own life so that I have time for Bible-reading,

?

[WHAT ARE THE
MARGINS
iN MY LIFE THAT
CREATE sacred
Space ?]

ANNIE DILLARD speaks to her fear of the blank page as a writer:

Who will teach me to write? A reader wanted to know.

The page, the page, the eternal blankness, the blankness of eternity which you cover slowly, affirming time's scrawl as a right and your daring as necessity; the page, which you cover woodenly, ruining it, but asserting your freedom and power to act, acknowledging that you ruin everything you touch but touching it nevertheless, because acting is better than being here in mere opacity; the page, which you cover slowly with the crabbed thread of your gut; the page in the purity of its possibilities; the page of your death, against which you pit such flawed excellences as you can muster with all your life's strength: that page which will teach you to write.

Drawing on her words, we might consider that the blank page is precisely what will teach us faith is that place where we are terrified to enter.

prayer, and marginalia-making. But after I make that first hard commitment to clear out an hour—or even half an hour—for prayer, then I find that finding the space in my own life is easier to do. What I learn about myself and God by slow Bible-reading and marginalia-making inspires me to find more and more frequent pockets of space in my life for prayer and Bible.

Creating space to even contemplate the edge is an act of daring in our over-full world. When life is too full, the first step in margin writing is to create a space to breathe and read and gain perspective. Even then, with that bold step, fear can still persist. Once we have space, we don't always know what to do with it. That space forces us to go deeper—within our heart and into the heart of God. Because we do not know and cannot control what we might unearth in that space, we avoid that sanctuary of sorts at all costs.

We fill our lives too full to the brim because we flee the broad range of emotions God asks us to engage. Do we have space for joy? Room for despair? The capacity to lament? The discipline of confession? A place to be refreshed?

If we can enter into the sacred space of the margins, then perhaps—with a little push from the divine secrets of harmonious page design—we might even find a place to dance lightly on the edges and design our lives accordingly.

Connecting with God

Ebenezer Yebuah

My wife Rejoice and I are from Ghana. We pray for our children—Ebenezer, Mawukle, Nan—while reading the Bible. We pray for them and write in the margins. We like to start with the Psalms and then begin to pray.

One psalm we love is Psalm 92:

> The righteous will spring up like a palm tree.
>   They will grow strong like a cedar of Lebanon.
> Those who have been replanted in the LORD's
>   house
>   will spring up in the courtyards of our God.
> They will bear fruit even when old and gray.
>   (Psalm 92:12-14a)

We pray our children will be like that palm tree. While we now live in Colorado, the palm tree reminds us of our home in Ghana.

Next to this passage, we have written our children's names. And we have written references to other passages, like Genesis 49:22 when Jacob prays for his children, and Deuteronomy 28:3 that begins, "You will be blessed in the city." These cross-references aid our prayer for their lives.

The palm tree is a common tree in Ghana where we are from—we use it for so many things—we can use the palm fruit for soup. We enjoy palm soup. You can use the juice from the palm as palm wine. You can use the leaves for firewood or as a shelter for a roof. And then, when you look at it, the palm is a plant that can stand all climate changes in our country. The palm tree represents faithfulness that is present in every season, like the palm tree is alive year round.

When you look at the roots of a palm tree, the roots penetrate deep into the ground. This is the prayer we have for the faith of our children. This symbolism means a lot to us. We are asking God to help our children be fruitful in this way—for the rest of their lives. This prayer begins in the margins of our Bible.

On the Pages of Your Bible

- Read Genesis 1, the story of creation. As you read, circle three "things" from creation that spark your imagination (stars, sea monsters, the sun). In the margin, scribble and sketch the creations you circled.

- Down the side of the page of Genesis 1, write the letters of the alphabet from A to Z. Take a deep breath and let your mind wander to the far corners of creation. What are you grateful for that starts with the letter A? B? C? Continue through until you reach the letter Z.

- Margin writing allows our character to be shaped by the textual imprint on the page. Hebrews 1:3 tells us:

  The Son is the light of God's glory and the imprint of God's being.

  What do we learn from this text about who God is? What might others learn from your character about the character of God? Fill up your margins with thoughts!

A GOD WHO WRITES
IN THE MARGINS

Give God the margin of eternity to justify himself.

[handwritten note: do i prefer margins justified or jagged? WHY so....??]

—*H. R. Haweis*

Perhaps Rich found the courage to venture into the margins because he believed in God who brings life abundant in the margins. From the beginning of creation God talks and all of life is mapped and named blessed.

I believe even God is a margin-writer. I believe God's script stretches across every edge of creation. Where there is laughter, God is writing in the margins. Where there is anguish, God is writing in the margins. God writes love letters in the margins. God writes even you and me into the margins of this crazy divine plan.

Consider this: on the first day of creation, before God picked up the pen to scribble in stars and moon, sun and sky (and the sea monsters of the deep); the Lord God looked at the margins around

and wondered what might come to life in those edges of existence. What we would see as void and empty, God saw as opportunity. Eugene Peterson, in *The Message*, describes it this way: "Earth was a soup of nothingness, a bottomless emptiness, an inky blackness" (Genesis 1:2).

Though faced with soup and nothingness, ink and emptiness, the formless void was not threatening but alive with possibility. Language, latent within those spaces, would be drawn out by the very breath, mind, and heart of the Lord God. By linking word to world, even now as formless void, the divine imagination could envision all of creation.

God's imagination is at peace even in the presence of the void, even when pushed to the edges of life. For the divine wisdom understood the hollow spaces could become hallowed. Just a few words needed to be written into the margins.

How incredible then, that our encouragement to engage God by writing in the margins might even be a reflection of the theological truth that we are created in the image of God. In creation, God wrote into the margins. And now, God nudges us to do the same.

God freely created as the universe came into being. Sometimes we have a hard time finding that freedom for our creativity. For that reason, take your pen or pencil into your nondominant hand. Read Genesis 2:4b-14 and let your hand draw this unfolding creation. Once you have finished your sketch, take a look and a deep breath. What do you notice about your picture that might not have occurred if you had used your dominant hand?

God Talk

So it would make sense that this God, the one who is the Alpha and Omega, the letter A and the letter Z, and every character in between, would have something profound to pen into place. This

God had something to say. For the difference between chaos and creative beauty is as simple as the singular word: good. As God talked in the margins, the context of the world came into being. As God talked in the margins, the intricate text of scripture came to life. As God talked in the margins, the subtext of human sin came into play. As God talked in the margins, word became flesh and the divine Word came to live and talk among us. From the beginning of creation, God had a few things to say.

The Holy Spirit burst into script. God couldn't wait to put words on the page. Dipping the pen into the inky blackness, the Lord God started to write, sketch, scribble, and draw. God's word became our world.

The blank pages of the universe were a canvas to all that God could create. The Lord God etched the curve of the horizon, the heights of the sky, the depths of the sea. Stars and sun, moon and meteorites filled the top of the pages.

Guiding that pen into the edges of existence, the Lord God created seed-bearing plants and fruit-bearing trees. Wild animals, cattle, reptiles, and bugs swarmed the ground. New life filled the margins.

After taking a deep breath, God looked around and noticed something important was missing.

> God created human beings;
> he created them godlike,
> Reflecting God's nature.
> He created them male and female.
>
> God blessed them:
> "Prosper! Reproduce! Fill Earth! Take charge!"
> (Genesis 1:27-28, *The Message*)

God was not interested in being the only writer. Prosper! Reproduce! Fill! God spoke to those the Lord had drawn and asked them to pick up a pen as well.

THE SPIRIT burst into script.... GOD'S WORD BECAME our world.

Add to the margins of this picture—it is not complete without your work too. Fill the earth, he says to them, add your script to this sacred text. Your flourishes, your script, your scribbles, even when you scratch things out, will help make my world complete. "I can't wait to see," offers the Lord God, "what you have to say as well." With those words God placed into the hands of humanity markers and crayons, pencils and pens, an array of neon highlighters and calligraphy pens.

Once God was finished to the very last detail, God put down the pen and rested. For a moment the page was complete. But still God had so much to say and so many blank spaces. For this God is the A to the Z: "I'm A to Z, the First and the Final, Beginning and Conclusion" (Revelation 22:13, *The Message*).

So full of potential writing, bursting to give greater expression! Not only does the Lord God encompass every letter of the alphabet, but nudges them into new margins and creates new meaning. The one who is the Alpha and Omega, the letter A through the letter Z, is the one who uses every letter in between to write the most sacred of stories. The intricate script of scripture is dictated by the one who can't be contained by every letter of the alphabet, so words burst forth and a new sentence is complete.

What does it look like when you start to do a little "God talk" in the margins? What is the first thing you want to say?

Life Maps

God's writing is in our hands. Scripture tells the story of this God who writes into the margins. As we turn the pages, God's hope is that we will map out our lives from the force and direction of these words. This script will save the world, redeem nations, overturn kingdoms, sustain breath, and draw out life even from death. The nouns and verbs, the adjectives and adverbs, the pronouns and participles, punctuation and paragraphs will take shape in our lives as we make the connections.

The problem is we miss them.

God keeps writing and we keep waiting, unable to see God at work again. The book of Job 9:9-11 in *The Message* explains it this way:

> *All by himself he stretches out the heavens*
> *and strides on the waves of the sea.*
> *He designed the Big Dipper and Orion,*
> *the Pleiades and Alpha Centauri.*
> *We'll never comprehend all the great things he does;*
> *his miracle-surprises can't be counted.*
> *Somehow, though he moves right in front of me, I don't see him;*
> *quietly but surely he's active, and I miss it.*

I'm tired of missing it. I want to see and comprehend those miracle-surprises as they occur in my life and the world around me. I'm hoping for a practice that helps me perfect the way I notice God as living and active. If God dipped a pen into that inky blackness, maybe there is an invitation for me to do the same by putting pen to page to "Prosper! Reproduce! Fill!"

When God bridged the distance between word and world, life happened. Now the invitation is ours to make the connections. With a hope we will venture into the blank spaces, pick up our pens, and draw forth life again; God sets us free. In the margins of that sacred text we have an opportunity to talk with God and map out our lives.

The map is provided through the lines of scripture. Proverbs 4:11 in *The Message* puts it this way, "I'm writing out clear directions to Wisdom Way, / I'm drawing a map to Righteous Road." Those God words provide clear direction and draw helpful maps, but our lives can be muddled and confused. We get lost in the context of biblical history; the words of the text don't always make sense. And then, there's the subtext of our own lives that always needs to be named, owned, confessed, and redeemed.

The margins offer an opportunity to sort all of that out. To put pen to paper and then, to pray in those blank spaces. Don't understand the story? Write the questions there. Wonder what this word really means? Write the definitions there. Lost in the muddled place of your own journey? Write those deep prayers there. Our empty spaces are God's possibilities.

The writing God sets things right, as the divine force faces the edges of life—the very margins of our existence—and through characters, strokes, and expression bridges word to world. When we read between the lines of that divine story, we are drawn into the script and find a greater story for the dramatic acts of our lives. Our prayers, etched alongside that story, draw us into God's play. As revelation upon revelation unfolds, God sets things right. God offers restoration alongside our prayerful inscriptions.

What if our own stories, our own personal days and dreams, hopes and hardships were written into that scroll? Every day was written, the psalm tells us and lets us see ourselves in the margins of God's incredible plan for creation.

Our work then, with pen and the prose of scripture, matters. As we write, we find new ways of living and engaging the world, new ways of imagining God's vision for the world, and new ways of understanding our responsibilities and roles within that place.

This is the work of the margins. In that inch we take note of revelation. In that inch we take note of the real and relevant stuff of our days. In that sacred edge, God's marginalia notes for *our* lives are realized.

As you sit, with pencil in hand and Bible in lap, at whatever edges of life you are living within, now that invitation is yours. Whatever chaos tugs at your heart and mind today, the creative practice of writing in the margins creates a divine conversation that transforms and guides. Meet God in the margins and let that revelation bring restoration to your life today. Let God shape your character from the textual imprint on the page. Let the font of scripture, typeset, and wellspring, be a place of nourishment and refreshment. Let God set things right in your life, and in this broken world, as you set out to write in the margins.

God laid out the world full of goodness and grace. As we look at the layout of our margins, with Bibles open in our laps, let us consider that crazy divine love.

Connecting with God

Agnes Nichols

As we quietly read our Bible, we find hearts that are noisy, anxious, and restless.

In Genesis 3 at the garden of Eden where I believe our whole being and who we are were formed, God banished Adam and Eve from the garden to work and wander all their days. We have been restless ever since.

In Matthew 8:20 (NRSV), after being questioned, Jesus answered: "Foxes have holes, and birds of the air have nests; but the Son of Man has nowhere to lay his head."

Animals have a place to return, a place to rest. Is it possible that even Jesus experienced this restlessness?

Was this Jesus' way of explaining what occurred in the garden of Eden? From that day humankind has been a nomadic people, wandering restlessly, seeking that elusive place.

Augustine said it this way in his *Confessions*, that we human beings,

go abroad to wander at the heights of mountains,
at the huge waves of the sea, at the long course of
the rivers,
at the vast compass of the ocean, at the circular
motion of the stars,
and pass by themselves without wondering.

I write in my margins to give my restlessness a place to land and to find in that space wisdom, truth, and love for daily living.

I wonder if the place where we might find our land and wonder is on the edge of the page. This is a place for our restless hearts to find their rest and to be called home.

On the Pages of Your Bible

- Luke 8:40-48 tells the story of a woman who touched the edge of Jesus' robe and received power. Reflect on this text in the edge of your Bible. What power lies within Jesus that is so strong that the woman might be healed even here at the edge?

- Job 26:7 offers a beautiful picture of God creating in the blank spaces. Sketch a picture of this image in the margin next to the text.

- Find a blank space in your Bible and write a prayer for blank spaces in your life.

- Second Samuel 6:14 speaks of David dancing before the ark. This moment marked the edge of something new that God was up to among the people of Israel. Rabindranath Tagore suggests we might dance on the edge of the page. What is God up to anew in your life that is worthy of a dance? Give thanks for that in the edge of the margin next to 2 Samuel 6:14.

- Why do you write in the margins of your Bible? Choose a blank space somewhere in your Bible, and write a "margin manifesto." Write your own mission statement in the margins. Turn to this upon occasion to remind yourself why this scriptural discipline is important to you.

A Few Definitions

In the realm of marginalia, naming a few definitions helps both for clarification and for encouraging new kinds of practices. Consider the following:

marginalia: Notes inscribed at the edge of the page. Sometimes the author offers marginalia to offer explanatory notes or commentary. Scholia, glosses, and annotations are margin notes made by the author. Sometimes the artist creates marginalia to illumine and explicate the text. Sometimes the reader creates marginalia in their own candid scribbles, revelations, and learned notes.

scholia: Instructive margin notes made by the author. These notes develop and interpret particular points, make reference to historical events, and refer to additional texts for consideration.

gloss: A margin note marking the definition of an obscure word. Similar to a glossary, but included within the margins of the page.

annotation: Margin notes made by the author that describe the author's thought process in producing the work. Sometimes these include corrections and addendums.

Illumination: An artist develops the text through image—including decorative borders, inscripted initials, and miniature paintings—in the margins of the biblical text. In the strictest sense, an illumination is used to define marginalia painting that includes gold or silver leaf.

common marginalia: Notes and candid scribbles made by the reader in the edge of the page that show an engagement and interface with the text. These notes represent the lively conversation developing between the reader and the text. The notes might include revelations, points of learning, questions, mnemonic devices, personal thoughts, ideas to remember. Marginalia makes visible the invisible, subconscious, and conversation unfolding.

MARGINALIA
AND MEMOS, SCHOLIA
AND SCRIBBLES

I never minded the random scribblings of other readers,
found them interesting in fact.
It is a truth universally acknowledged that people
write the darndest things in the margins of their books.

—Tara Bray Smith

No other time-honored spiritual practice is as immediate, raw, and engaged with scripture as writing—responding to God— in the margins of the Bible. Composers like Bach to theologians like Barth, botanists, and saints—all have engaged in personal and devotional ways with this practice. In doing so they engaged their fullest selves with our most significant text.

Each one of these margin notes or pictures or ancestries represents a saint, in the wide communion of saints, who hoped to live a

life of meaning in their pursuit of God. They read, they listened, they prayed, they wrote. Their margin notes are far from their last words. What we know of their lives is revealed in poems and hymns, paintings and professions, literature, and even in the surviving beauty of our natural world. So we will see here how these saints connected with God on the pages of their Bibles and then find inspiration for connecting with God on ours as well.

We learn from them how to lay out our lives from text to context and back to the text again. Their marginalia is testament to a way of reading, praying, writing, and living that we can all learn from.

Marginalia are simply words written on the pages of a printed text. Notes in the margins might be two words, a candid scribble, a structured annotation, an exclamation mark of revelation, the curvy journey of a question mark, or perhaps an inky rage. Along the borders of any given page, notes in the margins reveal the heart, mind, and soul. They reveal the spectrum of the heart's emotions, the engaged interaction with the ideas of the mind, and the soul's deepest prayers penned onto the page.

The word *marginalia* comes from the Latin word *margo*, meaning boundary, space, comfort, allowance, or cushion. Since the invention of the printing press, readers have kept their place as they read by pressing their thumbs in the margins. And for centuries, the margins have been a place for creative engagement. Monarch butterflies, Norwegian lemmings, the master of the playing cards, genealogies, hermit songs, and the origins of Bach cantatas share a singular similarity: they all appear as marginalia in Bibles.

The history of marginalia is lengthy and fascinating. This marginalia includes everything from annotations and cross-references printed in the Bible, to scholarly corrections or the scribe's correction in an illuminated text, to the genealogical and familial memories written into the Bible as history and testament, to personal notes written by famous people and ordinary people like you and me. A quick tour through the history of marginalia makes clear that the margins of a Bible can be a space for more than prayer lists or asterisks. Learning about this history helped expand my own sense of what I could write in my own Bible's margins. In the history of the church, people have filled their margins with just about every imaginable response to scripture (and, occasionally, with jottings that seem irrelevant to scripture)—and so can we!

Marginalia for a Communion of Saints

The Sea

Those are the two words that Herman Melville wrote next to Matthew 13:2—a verse in which Jesus is sitting in a boat on a lake, about to tell the parable of the sower. It was not the parable's rocky places or plants that leapt out at Melville, but something about Jesus' watery seat. Perhaps that marginal notation was the first seed of Melville's great sea-faring novel, *Moby Dick*.

Inscribed in the back of Melville's Bible is this quotation from St. Evremond:

> *Who well considers the Christian*
> *religion, would think that God*
> *meant to keep it in the dark*
> *from our understandings, and make*
> *it turn upon the motions of our*
> *hearts*

These words from Melville's Bible speak volumes. Melville cared about the ethics of Christian living, even though life is sometimes filled with the mystery and ambiguity of God. Never certain in his beliefs, struggling to ascertain wisdom for living was central to the spiritual quest of Herman Melville.

Art fills the pages of some Bibles, adding artists to the great legacy of marginalia contributors. Bibles like the Abbey Bible, the Luttrell Bible, and others use margin paintings to depict the ordi-

Marginalia is something like a small ship, a vessel, anchored for a moment across the vast sea of scripture. Perhaps the margin itself is like that shore where Christ anchors for a while and offers us teaching.

nary activities of everyday saints. The *Luttrell Psalter* is just one example of illuminations in the margins that provide us now with a glimpse into daily life in England during the medieval era. Through the paintings we discover the striking contrast between the life of the medieval Lord Luttrell and the numerous servants who tended his family and estate. Through the pages are images of servants feeding chickens, spouses fighting, cooking, and tending to sheep and other animals. The psalter has been noted for the dire look ever-present on the faces of the servants. As for Lord Luttrell, there are images of him mounted in full armor upon his horse and other images where he is present at the local church concerned about his afterlife.

This kind of quotidian margin drawing and writing has its place in our lives today. My friend Lauren tells me that when she is feeling overwhelmed by domestic and professional tasks, she turns to Proverbs 31 and lists the ways in which her tasks for the day are and are not like the woman of valor. "It helps me feel less overwhelmed to see that the Proverbs woman had a to-do list ten times as long," she tells me, "and it helps me think about my own tasks in a different frame. By setting my own professional to-do list down next to the Proverbs woman's vineyard planting and profitable trading, I am able to see my job not just as crushing stuff that I am behind on, but rather as something that may help me provide for my family and even the needy in my community."

Margins inform the everyday lives of writers and artists, as well as musicians, from the likes of Bach to Elvis who have been margin-writers as well.

In the 1830s Leonard Reichle's ancestors purchased a pile of old books in Philadelphia, one of them a Bible. A century later Reichle shared his family treasure with a visiting cousin, Lutheran pastor Christian Riedel. Upon opening the Bible, Riedel recognized the signature of a famous musician: Johann Sebastian Bach. Throughout the Bible more than three hundred marks in the text call attention to underlined passages, marks of emphasis, and statements written in the margins. Occasionally, the marginalia named a typographical or grammatical error. More often, the marginalia revealed notations linking text to lyrical insights and music. More than one thousand works for chorus and instruments find their genesis somewhere in Bach's Bible between Genesis and Revelation. The Calov Bible, as this Bible came to be called, shows more than three hundred touch points of musical inspiration. After being discovered by a pastor visiting his cousin, Bach's Bible now resides at the Concordia Seminary Library in St. Louis. The Bible was a three-volume Bible of the seventeenth century that also contains commentary by Martin Luther as well as theological reflections from a professor, Abraham Calovius.

In the Bible, next to 1 Chronicles 25, Bach penned, "This chapter is the true foundation of all God-pleasing church music." Beside 2 Chronicles 5:12-13 he wrote, "In devotional music, God is always present with his Grace."

When Thomas Rossin, a Minnesota conductor, saw the margins of Bach's Bible, he realized that any Bach performance should not be done in a large concert hall by a large and overpowering orchestra. Instead, he thought, "they should be done more intimately and from a faith perspective." The reason for this transition, according to Rossin, was Bach's love for God expressed in the edges and the deep faith formed at the margins.

Bach's Bible included notations that kept his scripture reading active, like in Exodus 38 where he calculates the measure of gold needed to build the Tabernacle and writes that number at the edge of the page. Throughout his Bible, it is clear that Bach struggled with the word *authority*. Not the authoritative grace of God, but the kinds of authority that seemed to cause conflict in his life with the church and city councils of Leipzig, Germany.

Exodus 15:20 is marked, "First prelude for two choirs to be sung to the glory of God." Next to Psalm 119:158, he wrote a "*nota bene*" or a "good word" to himself to take note so that he would truly hear and absorb the truth of the text, "I see the despiser and it grieves me that they do not keep your word." And he noted 1 Timothy 6:12 (NIV), "Fight the good fight of the faith. Take hold of the eternal life to which you were called when you made your good confession in the presence of many witnesses."

Sometimes, there are places where Bach underscored the words of Calovius. In one example, Bach highlights: "My hymn sounds like this: Give to God the glory which is due to the one true living God, the only glory, praise and honor in heaven and on earth." In these annotations we see Bach looked to the sacred word of the text, in his scriptural disciplines, to find both inspiration and a solid foundation for all his life's work.

In Bach's annotations we see the markings of a great mind and musician at work. For this, Bach looked to the sacred word of text in his scriptural practice to find direction for his anger, momentum for his music, absolution for his sin, and dictums to guide his life. Bach's scribbles provide direction for our scriptural disciplines. Bach's text is the museum piece that begs to be seen and viewed as holy. His is not scandal, but sumptuous love that breaks forth in sacred song.

What we see in Bach's Bible is that back-and-forth between insight and life work, the verse of the Bible, and the vocation of our lives.

Even Elvis prayed in the margins of his Bible. While writing these pages, the sale of Elvis's Bible, complete with margin notes, made headline news. In 1957, Elvis received a new Bible for Christmas from his Uncle Vester and Aunt Clettes.

One margin note offers a glimpse into his life of prayer:

There is a season for everything. Patience will reward you and reveal all answers to your questions.

ELVIS' marginal Notes!

*

Scribbled across a bottom margin in Luke's Gospel, Elvis wrote, *"Lead me, guide me in all your ways."* The note is significant in its link to one of Elvis's famous songs, "Lead Me, Guide Me."

Perhaps most poignant is one of the notes scrawled in the back of the Bible:

To judge a man by his weakest link or deed is like judging the power of the ocean by one wave.

This vestige of Elvis's prayer life remains as an insight and witness to his life of faith. And it is an inspiration to us to let God lead us, and guide us, through our lives.

Connecting with God

How incredible that this communion of saints finds direction in the margins. We see in their legacy incredible connections to God that help us, through their work, to find a deeper connection to God as well.

Of course, sometimes finding that elusive "connection to God" means being honest about the disconnect.

Prior to the invention of the printing press, Bibles were hand-copied by monks in their monasteries. Those medieval Bibles make clear that people have always drawn connections (indeed, literally drawn them) between biblical stories and their own contexts. Sometimes the monks who copied the Bibles themselves made notes in the margins.

"Let the reader's voice honor the writer's pen," wrote one monk.

"And, Oh reader, take note. While the hand that copied this text molders in the grave . . . the Word copied lives forever!" These were instructions of a sort to those who would read the text, urging the reader to honor the Scriptures and to honor the labor that went into producing the hand-copied manuscript. Are they so different from the marginal notes I find printed in my *Women's Devotional Bible*— or in the note I wrote in the Bible I gave a teenager at her confirmation, wishing her a fruitful life in the Word and in the Spirit?

A recent article by Maria Popova tells of monks complaining in the margins of their illuminated texts:

New parchment, bad ink. I say nothing more.
I am very cold.
Thank God it's getting dark.
As the harbor is welcome to the sailor, so is the last line to the
scribe.

When I first read these gripes, I was a little taken aback—I picture the monastic labor of copying Holy Scripture as a very sacred task. But upon reflection, I thought, well, why not? Why shouldn't the Scriptures be the place we also lay out our frustrations with our daily work, even—perhaps especially—if that work is "religious" in nature?

I bet there is more than one pastor who, after a particularly trying day at work, has made an exclamation mark or two next to Numbers 11:10-15, in which the Israelites are complaining endlessly about their lack of meat, and Moses, fed up with their grousing, in turn grouses to God, saying,

Why have you treated your servant so badly? And why haven't I
found favor in your eyes, for you have placed the burden of all these
people on me? . . . Where am I to get meat for all these people?
They are crying before me and saying, "Give us meat, so we can
eat." . . . If you're going to treat me like this, please kill me.

Sometimes a practice as simple as naming the disconnect eases us closer to that elusive connection.

Some of what emerges from the array of marginalia is real, pointed insights into history. These historical connections help us to understand divine connections in a variety of different decades. We see the struggle of a people, and their solace. We see their discoveries and learn of the adventures we might take for granted.

In a French Bible from the fourteenth century, there is a simple sketch of a finger pointing to 2 Samuel 24:15 with "So the Lᴏʀᴅ sent a plague on Israel from that very morning until the allotted time. Seventy thousand people died, from Dan to Beer-sheba." Why was this text meaningful to the reader? Because he lived during the explosion of the Black Plague, which took, like Samuel's pestilence, thousands upon thousands of lives. With a simple drawing the reader of this text invited a biblical text into his own time and place.

In 1516 Agostino Giustiniani published in Genoa a psalter with the first published history of Columbus's discovery of the new world in 1492. Next to Psalm 19:4, "their words reach the ends of the earth," Giustiniani added a quite lengthy marginal note explaining that Christopher Columbus, a son of Genoa, had fulfilled this scripture by exploring more sea and land than anyone of his day and age. He had discovered "the ends of the earth" as noted in the psalm, thereby fulfilling the promise of scripture. This marginal note is of historical importance for its naming of Columbus's mission.

How incredible that we learn this history through the margins.

We also learn of incredible landscapes, in particular places and times, through the margins. Painted illuminations and scientific notations help us see divine connections come alive through the eyes of individuals.

Even today, monks in Minnesota are illuminating what has come to be called The Saint John's Bible. Their illuminations, like those from centuries past, include flora and fauna, butterflies and insects, painted into the page to create beauty and root the scripture in the landscape of a particular place. Their paintings remind me of my friend Betsy who looks out the window of her kitchen and is thrilled to see the first buds and birds of spring. She sketches them next to the Psalms in her Bible. I love her for this.

The Saint John's Bible aims to be an illuminated Bible for the twenty-first century. Such a project allows all the discoveries of past centuries to be depicted in the illuminations. So the double helix of the DNA, photos from the Hubble telescope, voice lines from cultures across the world, tapestries, weavings, and ancient cave painting images recently discovered fill the illuminations. These images help readers grasp how this ancient text is connected to, and relevant for, our modern era.

I love the images of Monarch butterflies that fill the margins at the end of Mark's Gospel in The Saint John's Bible. The Gospel of Mark is cryptic in its telling of the Resurrection. The earliest manuscripts leave the details to our imagination. Marginalia allows the illustrator to fill in what some say seem to be missing from the end of Mark's Gospel: the Resurrection. Some scholars believe the original ending concludes with verse 8 and the fear of the stunned women at the empty tomb. By using the symbolism of the caterpillar, chrysalis, and butterfly, the artists illuminate the transformation that occurs in the risen Jesus of the Resurrection. Suggesting something far beyond any words can say, these pictures are worth a thousand views.

The Saint John's Bible also includes corrections; when a scribe drops a line, clever illustrations call the reader's attention to the bottom of the page to pick up the line that has been dropped. For example, an image of pulleys and ropes lifts up the omitted line from the bottom of the page and drags it to the point in the text where it should occur. These frank admissions of error may be my favorite marginalia ever. They make me more forgiving of my own errors (errors I have made in marginalia, but more important, errors I have made in my life), and remind me that I can find God even in the midst of making, and correcting, a mistake.

In Norway, researchers took notes at one point in the margin of a Bible to correct the ecological mistakes of a struggling environment. In their margins, they studied the decline of the lemming population and searched the margins of local Bibles. Lemmings are critical to the ecosystem; but recent years have shown a sharp decline in their usual population growth. Writings in the margins of Bibles over the years have documented years of high and low lemming outbreaks. In the texts describing the plague of locusts,

... REMIND ME THAT I CAN FIND GOD EVEN IN THE MIDST OF MAKING, & CORRECTING, A MISTAKE.

Norwegians have been known to scratch out locusts and write in lemming counts.

How amazing, really, to see the vocation of writers and musicians, artists and scientists come to life in the way they connect to God on the pages of their Bibles.

Sometimes the margins provide a place to validate and direct a person's vocational life. Next to Genesis 45:5, in the Bible of Florence Nightingale, is written, "God did send me to preserve life." Many of the other notes in her Bible mark the thought process of a critical thinker, someone not willing to take at face value the direct words on the page. And yet, in this moment of clarity, we see a glimpse into her self-revelation of personal vocation. Connecting her life's call, to the story of Joseph in Egypt, she finds clarity that God works through humanity to offer saving grace.

Since I learned of Nightingale's vocational note-taking, I have found myself making marginal notes about my own vocation in my Bible, musing after reading the burning bush or Jesus' call to the disciples to drop their nets and follow him, about the ways I am, and am not, following God in my work life.

Jason Byassee a United Methodist pastor and author, prayed in his margins before going to college. Next to Colossians 2:8, "See to it that nobody enslaves you with philosophy and foolish deception, which conform to human traditions and the way the world thinks and acts rather than Christ" he wrote: "Watch out for college." His story reminds us that we stay connected to God by praying about our vocations, and our passions, and by asking God to steady us along life's crazy way.

On the Pages of Their Bibles

The pages of their Bibles, the pages of our Bibles, reveals the lives of saints who simply want to dwell in the presence of God.

Each page tells the story of a prayer, a hope, a day in the life of an ordinary saint.

The pages of their Bibles often tell the story of a family's history, especially back in the day when paper was scarce and Bibles were a precious resource. Many can tell the story of an important Bible in their family system. Maybe your Bible will be that precious one as the future unfolds.

In Alabama's Cherokee County, a discovery of the Daniel family Bible is an invaluable resource for genealogy. Marked with twenty surnames: Byrne, Daniel, Dibrell, Harrison, Jackson, Lawler, Maddin, Mahew, McDowell, McFearen, Mead, Money, Morring, Penny, Sawrie, Spriggs, Sullivan, Tipton, Woodward, and Wortham; the discovery provides a wealth of information. In days when paper was scarce, the family Bible served as a portable history. The Daniel family Bible records seven weddings, fifteen deaths, and more than thirty births dating back to 1832.

This Bible is recorded within an incredible database of Bibles. Hundreds of family Bible records are maintained in a database where access to lists of weddings, funerals, and baptisms are easily accessed. Notes from the Bibles, scans of the pages, and lists of the genealogies are all available. This is a place to explore the last names within your family system to follow the lineage and unpack genealogical insights. The Bibles of Cherokee County, Alabama, are a particular listing on this site to document the fascinating history of this part of the country.

Further up the East Coast, another story is told. The pages of a Bible from Martha's Vineyard not only tell the family history of the Wampanoag tribe of Native Americans, but also, in the end, the history that helped to preserve their language that was about to be lost.

There, a Bible now stored in a library in Philadelphia, reveals lines written in the Wampanoag language of the early Native American community and provides a cryptic key into their nearly lost language. In this Bible, John Eliot, an early preacher, gained the ability to speak—and thereby, minister—across communities.

Recently the Wampanoag language gained attention when Jessie Little Doe Baird received the MacArthur Foundation genius prize for her work in recovering this long-silenced language. Through her work in the texts of this Bible and through the marginal notes, she gleaned insights into this language. What had been considered "marginal," this lost language gained recognition and honor through its recovery in the margins.

What if we all could recall an original language, an elemental language, that language of deep connection to God through the margins of our Bibles?

Marginalia is a broad and varied topic. Johann Sebastian Bach wrote into the margins of his Bible. So did, perhaps, your grandmother. While Bach's marginalia is famous and priceless, your grandmother's Bible notes might hold secrets to your family's history that would otherwise go untold. The notes that are more fleeting, scattered, and perhaps in the end, more insightful are the margin notes inscripted onto a page in pen or pencil by a wide range of people throughout the years.

Bible margins contain drawings of monarch butterflies, notes on the Norwegian lemming population, long lost genealogies, first drafts of hermit songs, and insights into Bach cantatas. Baptisms are recorded in the margins. First communions. Weddings. Deaths. And always, prayers.

Connecting with God

Allison Agnew

there are
two types of folks in this old world

those who like to keep their books
pristine
clean
and underline free
with pages crisp and new

and then there are the rest of us

who scribble
jot
underscore
and highlight

meaningful words
useful ideas
needful passages to commit to memory

we turn down pages
and leave our books
tented open
with cracked spines

and those Bibles
leave a trail of breadcrumbs
of our spiritual journey

a kind of road map
for those who will read them later

On the Pages of Your Bible

- Turn to Mark 16. Take note of the various endings. Doodle a few butterflies in the margins to remind you of the Resurrection as represented in The Saint John's Bible. Write a prayer about resurrection life to guide you as well.

- Turn to Exodus 10, the plague of locusts. Scratch out the word *locust* and write something from your native area that plagues your community. How was God using the plagues to get the attention of Pharaoh? Write a prayer in the margin.

- Turn to Luke 1:46-55. This is Mary's song, the Magnificat. Note in the margins: What instruments would you use to help your contemporaries hear this song? What lyrics would you highlight? What group would you like to hear do a rendition of this song? What would its chorus be? This is a biblical text that calls for deep changes in the world. Write a few petitions for what might need to be turned upside down in the world around us.

- Turn to Matthew 1, the genealogy of Jesus. In the margins, jot down your genealogy as far back as you can remember. How does God use genealogies to speak to us? What is the point of the genealogy of Jesus? What is the hope of your genealogy?

- Florence Nightingale finds an insight into her vocation next to Genesis 45:5, where she wrote, "God did send me to preserve life." What insight about your particular calling would you write in your margin?

CONNECTING WORD TO WORLD: PRAYING THE HORIZONTAL AND THE VERTICAL

Margin space, which we typically think of as narrow, insignificant space, is actually a vital interpretive e dge that enlivens the pages of tradition. The margins represent the very space upon which the book's life is dependent.

—Terry Veling

After reading and listening, we pause. We let the blank space of the margins around the edge of the page give us room to breathe. Then we begin making connections. As our eye skims the margins across the top and bottom of the page, we begin praying how the words from the text might meet our own context. What does the horizon of this text have to do with the horizons of our days?

At the same time, we get to praying vertically. The margin space on the left and the right, inch our eyes up and down from heaven to earth. Here is a place of divine connection. We get to praying vertically as we breathe in this space and talk with God.

Praying Horizontally

Two days after 9/11, my friend Rich opened his Bible and read Proverbs 2:

> *My son, accept my words*
>> *and store up my commands.*
> *Turn your ear toward wisdom,*
>> *and stretch your mind toward understanding.*
> *Call out for insight,*
>> *and cry aloud for understanding.*
> *Seek it like silver;*
>> *search for it like hidden treasure.*
> *Then you will understand the fear of the LORD,*
>> *and discover the knowledge of God.*
> *The LORD gives wisdom;*
>> *from his mouth come knowledge and understanding.*
> *He reserves ability for those with integrity.*

And then Rich asked in his margin, "What are you preparing me for, God?" Rich was praying for personal direction to move from the words and assurance of the scriptural text out into the world spinning in a whole new context.

Why write in the margins? Because engaging that one-inch margin of the page is a discipline of moving from word to world and back again. There in that one-inch margin separating word and world we find meaningful connections by digging deeper into the

TWO FOCI:

① HORIZONTAL
(horizon of our daily lives)

② VERTICAL
(praying vertically — our connection with God)

INTERSECTION
(combined prayer & living)

information supplied in the text and the formation scripture has for us and for our world.

The resolution Rich came to is revealed on the page. *What are you preparing me for?* Rich wrote the answer he heard through prayer: *To make others more great.*

Moving from word to world is a central task of praying in the margin. We engage the text on the margin; and then we move either physically or mentally into the world about us. When Rich sat with that Bible on his lap during those eerily blue sky days in September more than a decade ago, the single thing that separated God's word from his world was that one-inch margin. This is precisely the place where Rich sought to make sense of the world.

The horizontal expanse across the bottom of the page serves as a vast space to draw in the horizons of our lives. What is going on in the world around us? What are we experiencing on the horizons of our days? Write that into the bottom of the page. This is the horizon of our living.

For Rich, notes about the horizon of his personal life of marriage and work fill the tops and bottoms of the page. *Praying for leadership development.* In addition, notes and prayers for our world are tucked in as well. *Pray for free elections in Iraq.* Rich prayed daily for this world to be just a bit better. His words, *What are you preparing me for?* is a prayer that utters, "I'm reading your word here, Lord. I know our complicated world. Help me make sense of my particular mission." The margins help us make connections between word and world to create a vision statement for living. We need that statement of purpose to emerge from the pages of our Bibles so we can live new horizons.

Funny that the only difference between "word" and "world" is that single stroke of the letter "l." Just like the vertical margin on the right side of the page, that "l" provides an inch of space. We discover that inch of space when we still our hearts, sit in the sanctuary, enjoy a sacred space outdoors, or have a long conversation with a trusted friend. But we also find that slice of heaven, that bit

the horizon of our living.

WOR(L)D
word vs. world

of breathing room, that margin to consider in the edges of scripture. This margin, that stroke of "l" is the distance from word to world.

And then, when the horizon of our world looks dim, when we need help connecting this word to our world, then we begin to pray that vertical edge.

Praying the Vertical

The vertical reminds me of the wisdom that comes from above, straight down to the ground upon which I stand. In that vertical inch of space, I am reminded of those divine intersections and the way that God pierces our hearts through revelation. Here, I jot notes that matter regarding the wisdom from the text and what that wisdom means for my way of living.

The vertical expanse, down the page, then becomes the place where God's divine word descends and enters our hearts and world. This is the place for naming the truth of the text. Instructions for living revealed in scripture go in this space. Here, we write out what we learn from the story of scripture.

Danny Coleman does this discipline well. Down the right side of the margins in his Bible are incredible notes on the structure and intent of each text. Down the right margin of John's Gospel he notes:

Emphasis on Jesus as God. Not as linear as other Gospels.
Revolves around "Seven miracles" and "Seven I am statements."
Purpose is to show that Jesus is the Son of God.

These words orient the lens through which he reads every word on this page and the next. His Bible study is not written into another notebook, but here, on the page where the words come to life and create a structure within which to understand the story.

Norman Vincent Peale tells a story of seeing what is reported

*vertical expanse where God's divine word descends

to be one of Abraham Lincoln's Bibles used during the Civil War. While Peale flipped through the pages, he came across an indentation and smudge mark in the margin next to Psalm 34:4. One would presume that Lincoln, the great freedom writer of the Civil War, found wisdom and freedom from fear there on the edge of the page. The verse he must have read often is an earnest prayer for freedom from fear: *I sought the Lord and he heard me. He delivered me from all my fears.* Lincoln "prayed the vertical" by simply pressing his thumb into that vertical margin and praying for strength.

For Lincoln, the words on the page and that inch of space to the right created a respite from the difficult world in which he lived. In that inch, he gained perspective, strength, and perseverance for the arduous journey ahead. Each time he came back to that text, he pressed his thumb into the page to reorient after experiencing the disorienting whirl of the world. The inch provides a place for coming and going, for orienting after getting disoriented, for finding a strong foundation after losing ground. Then, strengthened, Lincoln reentered the world to live out the vision he discovered in scripture.

Finding Meaning at the Intersection of the Vertical and the Horizontal

Of course, the cross is the clearest picture of the horizontal meeting the vertical, where the broken world horizon of our world is intersected with that vertical and transcendent grace of God.

Occasionally, in our own lives we experience those transforming and sacred intersections.

During college, I often questioned whether I was in the right place, doing the right thing. One weekend, I went on a college retreat for Christian students in Harlem, New York. We had been to the Abyssinian Baptist Church to worship. We had eaten at Sylvia's. We roamed the gardens at the Cathedral of St. John the Divine.

Amid all this beauty, there was still an ache in my heart. I wasn't sure I was in the right place doing the right thing. My restless heart kept me from the sense of rootedness that was my deepest prayer.

That night, our leaders asked us to open our Bibles to Jeremiah 29:11-13, and then we read these verses:

I know the plans I have in mind for you, declares the LORD;
they are plans for peace, not disaster, to give you a future
filled with hope. When you call me and come and pray to me,
I will listen to you. When you search for me, yes, search for me with
all your heart, you will find me.

Was it possible these words were written just for me? How did they so clearly name my deepest sighs and my unspoken prayers? While countless others across space and time have found meaning in these words written to a community in exile, for this moment, they were mine and they mattered. These words intersected my very core. They knew the content of my life and with that sacred intersection began to reshape that content into a new purpose and a renewed hope.

I have no doubt that countless Bibles have marginal notes next to Jeremiah 29. I've met many people who have opened their Bibles and shown me just that text. But for me, on that balmy night in Harlem, those words were intimately mine. How is it that scripture speaks so personally to us, and yet so universally to all people, in all places, and at all times?

There—on the horizon of my life—the divine word from God descended like a vertical ladder to ease me slowly to a new place.

This is the secret that Rich Gordon and Abraham Lincoln knew: sacred intersections can happen in the margins when we let our horizontal lives meet God's vertical dimension of transforming grace.

"
I KNOW THE PLANS I
HAVE IN MIND FOR YOU,
declares the LORD;
THEY ARE PLANS FOR
PEACE, NOT DISASTER,
TO GIVE YOU A FUTURE
filled w/ **HOPE**.
"
JEREMIAH 29

Connecting with God

Alex Taylor

This summer I found myself in a whole new world. Having grown up in small town, New Wilmington, Pennsylvania, I went away for the first time to live three blocks from the sand, waves, and boardwalk of Ocean City, New Jersey. And instead of babysitting, I worked at a frozen yogurt store called "Peace, Love, and Yogurt."

In this place, I found myself in a whole new world of feelings. I had never lived in a community filled with people intensively following their passion and yearning for Christ. So, that summer for me was one of simply and radically feeling set free. To me, God has always been a huge part of my life. But my faith had not guided my entire life. I wasn't willing to give God every circumstance of my life. One aspect in particular was relationships with others. I am definitely a people pleaser, never wanting to hurt or disappoint anyone. I have a hard time surrendering circumstances to others, as well as trials that I face to God. I never considered myself to be prideful, but that summer I realized just how independent I thought I could be, but how completely broken and dependent on Him that I truly am. Although this fear may have allowed me to keep in good standing with a lot of earthly things, I have been paralyzed from living for eternity.

In this new world, I really relied on God's word.

Although I grew up in the church, I had never been a part of a Bible study or group that actually studied the Bible. Moreover, we actually discussed a book after we had read it. Although these were definitely fruitful experiences, I learned at the beach just how dependent I was on His word in shaping who I am meant to become. It finally made sense to me that summer that I wasn't here, just left to wander around in this world, but rather to explore this world based on the word stated so clearly in the Bible.

I suddenly couldn't get enough of scripture and what He would reveal to me. That summer we studied the Gospel of Mark in our small groups. Throughout the summer, one of the main verses of Mark that influenced me from the start was Mark 4:40, "But He said to them, 'Why are you so fearful? How is that you have no faith?'" (NKJV). As I mentioned earlier, fear is paralyzing. I too often forget that the God who created the universe, who sent His son to die for us, is the One in control. Why wouldn't I put my faith in Him? Next to the story of the wind and the waves obeying Jesus (Mark 3:35-39), I have written, "May not be immediate results . . . but Have Faith" and "Lift things up to God with an open hand, not a closed fist" (Romans 5:3-6).

On the Pages of Your Bible

- Martin Buber says, "All real living is meeting." Call three friends or family members and ask them their favorite scripture. Turn to the texts, then pray in the margins using the words of the scripture for this friend or family member.

- Consider the vertical margin as a place to write down revelations from God's "word." Consider the horizontal margin as a place to write down sighs and joys from our "world." Practice a scriptural discipline of writing down your "learning" from the text in the vertical. Pen prayers and reflections from your life in the horizontal.

- Matthew 6:9-13 provides the prayer that Jesus taught us. Here, Jesus teaches us to pray, "Your kingdom come, your will be done, on earth as it is in heaven." Consider Veling's phrase that the margins provide "millions of moments of encounter." Write in your margin prayers for heaven meeting earth, and earth meeting heaven.

- When reading narratives, one way to get into the world of feelings within those words is through an exercise in Bible drama. After reading a sentence or two of the narrative, ask yourself— "Who am I?" and "What am I feeling?" Write that in the margin, then continue the story and ask again.

- Proverbs 2:7 is a text that mattered to Rich. Consider the words "ability" and "integrity." In the margin, write a prayer offering your abilities to God. Then, write a second stanza of prayer for your personal integrity before God and neighbor.

- In your Bible, next to Psalm 34:4 write, "Abraham Lincoln's Prayer." Now, write a prayer asking God for a transformation of your own fears.

- In his Bible, Rich asked, "God, what are you preparing me for?" Turn to these texts that speak to being prepared. Choose one. Then journal in the margin about its meaning to you.

Jeremiah 1:5 1 Corinthians 16:13 Hebrews 11:7

1 Peter 3:15 John 14:3 2 Timothy 4:2

PRAYING IN THAT INCH OF SPACE

Next to Revelation 22:
I was reading this Bible at my barracks at 10:40
Tuesday, June 4, 1918
and prayed to be at home.
So I hope to be home before long.

—*Arthur R. Walls, South Fork, Pa., Cambria Co.*

Prayer Lines

Sometimes marginalia is as simple as a line down the page.
That is exactly what is scrawled down the right-hand margin
of my friend Mike's Bible next to Matthew 7:7-12.

Ask, and you will receive. Search, and you will find. Knock,
and the door will be opened to you. For everyone who asks,

receives. Whoever seeks, finds. And to everyone who knocks, the
door is opened. Who among you will give your children a stone
when they ask for bread? Or give them a snake when they ask
for fish? If you who are evil know how to give good gifts to your
children, how much more will your heavenly Father give good
things to those who ask him. Therefore, you should treat people
in the same way that you want people to treat you; this is the
Law and the Prophets.

For more than twenty years Mike's addiction to prescription painkillers and alcohol kept him in the streets and estranged from his family. One sunny October day, Mike checked himself into the local city rescue mission. With a friend from the streets, the two pledged to get sober together. Early in the treatment, Mike learned this text from one of the chaplains. Down the side of his Bible he scrawled a single line to mark the text. For the next four years, these words marked by this line became a daily prayer.

One night, a few months into the program, Mike walked in the yard outside the mission praying this text aloud. The night was beautiful, filled with stars, and Mike turned his head heavenward as he prayed the words. When a car pulled up beside him, he was caught off guard. In the vehicle was a policeman, concerned about this guy seemingly talking to himself.

"Are you all right?" the cop asked Mike. Mike laughed to himself, knowing he was the most all right he had been in decades. He said to the policeman, "I'm talking to the guy upstairs."

That prayer, for Mike, began in the margins of his rescue mission Bible next to Matthew 7. The single line, etched as a prayer in the margin, was working to help inch Mike into new ways of living, freed from past addiction. This line, next to this text, needed to move mountains and open up new pathways for living.

Avenues of Prayer

Our margins are avenues for prayer. They inch us into new ways of living and moving and centering our very being. The prayers that take place in that space are sometimes very specific and other times full of generalities.

A friend tells the story of his grandfather's Bible. The prayers written into the margins, circled in the text and the words standing out in bold name a single spiritual gift that is prayed for repeatedly: patience.

The family smiles now when they flip through the pages of his Bible, knowing the ease of his impatience, they see in the pages an earnest prayer for transformation. Somehow, the margins provide a place for grace and perspective. Not only did the margins shape the prayer life of the grandfather, but also, in some ways the margins even now shape the prayers of his descendants as they come to peace with his life and legacy.

Kalyn is a young woman who has known hardship and has written next to Exodus 16 (the story of manna and quail), as a personal reminder, *"The Lord's provisions are sufficient even when I want more."* Knowing the grief that Kalyn has experienced in her life, I want more for her as well. Still, she centers herself for living for God with this prayer written in that inch of space.

In the margins, we name specific petitions we have before God in prayer. Rich's Bible was filled with them: Patience. Leadership. Reconciliation. Love. Surrender.

This is the place, where as Dawson Trotman says, "Thoughts disentangle themselves as they pass over our lips and through our fingertips." Prayers named, spoken, and penned begin to untangle our minds, unravel our confusions, and unknot the tied-up spots in our hearts and souls. We live into patience. We lean into God's provision. We get disentangled. We petition God to find our way home. We practice new ways of living.

We pray.

THOUGHTS

Pathways for Prayer

Sometimes our prayers are known and easily named. We need patience, now! and know it. With that, we pen into the margins that prayer for patience. But sometimes we need to create the space, through disciplines of prayer, that allows us to live into prayers yet unnamed and not yet known.

My friend Betsy Boyd, a creative margin-writer, told me she writes and doodles and scribbles many mornings to pray. She collects her thoughts for the morning, those thoughts scattered after yesterday's demands. She reads. She looks for what stands out in bold to her. She underlines the text. She squiggles wavy lines across the bottom margin of the page. She picks up her pen. She writes the words of the text, like Romans 15:13, in between the squiggly lines so there is a particular cadence to the enlarging and shrinking the words of the text. She grabs a few markers or colored pencils and colors in the shapes that emerge. Once the margin is complete the scripture text has been etched into her heart and mind for the day just as it reverberates on the edge of the page. Now, she knows Romans 15:13: "May the God of hope fill you with all joy and peace in faith so that you overflow with hope by the power of the Holy Spirit."

The verse is imprinted on her heart, mind, and soul. And as the day's needs arise, words pop up from the margins of the Bible into the edges of her day: Peace. Hope. Joy. Overflow. Power. Just what Betsy needs for the living and loving of her days.

Funny to think that Betsy writes for many of the same reasons Jesus may have scribbled in the sand. She honors the law. She names sins. She gains composure. She takes a deep breath. She cross-references texts. She solves problems. She comes to unexpected answers in that unexpected space. She unearths grace.

Why do you write in the margins of your Bible?

What's wonderful about the margins is their potential for discovery, creativity, and daily joy. The margins offer a place for faith to develop in clarity and deepen in mystery. The margins offer a place for hope to gain security, grace to gain awareness, and wisdom to find its ground. The margins are a place for love to be nurtured into actuality.

The Christian tradition offers many pathways for prayer. Here, we'll explore a few avenues that have held meaning for saints and sinners throughout the years. We'll take these ancient practices for prayer into the margins to inch into new ways of praying.

The Wesleyan Quadrilateral

Consider the guidelines used for discernment in the Methodist tradition, the Wesleyan Quadrilateral. The quadrilateral offers four lines of illumination through scripture, tradition, experience, and reason. The United Methodist Church affirms, "Wesley believed that the living core of the Christian faith was revealed in Scripture, illumined by tradition, vivified in personal experience, and confirmed by reason. Scripture [however] is primary, revealing the Word of God 'so far as it is necessary for our salvation.'"

The margins offer a great space for laying out this quadrilateral. After turning to a text you hope to explore, write these four words across the four outer margins from the left edge, across the top, to the right edge, and across the bottom: "Scripture," "Tradition," "Experience," and "Reason."

First, read the text and write in the margin marked "Scripture" the key touchstones for faith you discovered in this text. Second, in the margin marked "Tradition," explore this text in commentaries, Bible dictionaries, and online commentaries. What does the history of Christian scholarship offer in response to this text? Third, in the margin marked "Experience," consider the response for commonsense Christianity. What would your grandmother take from this text? What would your neighbor wonder about it? What would the person in the pew beside you gain for living from this passage?

Finally, in the fourth margin marked "Reason," consider how this text engages the Holy Spirit in your life. Scripture engages our vital, lived Christian experience. What do you bring from your experience to this text? What do you bring from this text for your experience?

The Wesleyan Quadrilateral offers a beautiful way to use the margins on every page. The four questions for scripture, tradition, experience, and reason create a great balance between the text, your context, the wisdom of the past, and the concerns of the everyday Christian. Together, these four reflections create a full and measured response to any given Bible passage.

Meditating on the Word

In the Presbyterian tradition, the *Directory for Worship* offers a wealth of wisdom for why we might write and pray in response to scripture. Naming scripture as the center of our worship and personal discipleship, the directory then offers some avenues for creative engagement:

> *One may meditate upon the Word by,*

> 1. *committing passages of Scripture to memory,*
> 2. *recalling and reflecting upon the revelation of God,*
> 3. *analyzing and comparing biblical themes, images, and forms,*
> 4. *finding touch points and exploring relationships between Scripture and life,*
> 5. *entering imaginatively into the world and events portrayed in the Bible to participate in what God does and promises there,*
> 6. *wrestling with the challenges and demands of the*
> 7. *offering one's self afresh for life in response to God.*

COMMIT
RECALL
ANALYZE
ENTER
FIND
WRESTLE
OFFER

It is often helpful to keep a record of one's insights and personal responses to reading, studying, and meditating upon the Word, or to share them with others. Writing paraphrases, summaries, and brief reflections, making creative responses, and keeping journals are all disciplines that assist in responding to the Word of God in Scripture. It is especially important in personal worship to read widely in Scripture. Using lectionaries and various translations and paraphrases is helpful in seeking to hear the full message of God's Word.

Why do we write? The Presbyterian tradition names wonderful active verbs as an answer: to commit, to recall, to analyze, to find, to enter, to wrestle, and to offer. These are all forms of prayer.

Breehan, an amazing photographer and athletic coach in my town, tells a margin story of "meditating" on a path of scriptures through the book of Romans. She says:

There are a series of passages to walk you to salvation starting with Romans 3:10-12 and concluding with Romans 8:38-39. I have these marked in my Bible, as I know many other Christians do.

P-R-A-Y

A simple acrostic for prayer is this: Praise, Remember, Ask, Yield. These four touchstones can be marked in the four edges of your margins. Write "praise" on the left edge, "remember" across the top, "ask" down the right edge, and "yield" across the bottom. The fourfold invitation is this: Praise God for any given thing in your life or the larger world right now. Remember how God has been faithful to you, your church, and the life of the world by denoting specific moments of God's presence. Ask God for specific petitions for your life, your neighbor's life, and for the nations. Yield to God, give up control, and place into God's hands all your needs, hopes, and desires.

A friend yielded in a life-giving way through that acronym to P-R-A-Y. She says:

> *Luke 12:25-26 is underlined and in the margin I wrote*
> *BE CONTENT !*

Prayer of St. Ignatius

Another saint of the church who has taught us to pray is Ignatius of Loyola. He offered his community a mode of praying called *examen*, which involves asking reflective questions at the end of each day:

> *What was the challenge of your day?*
> *What was the blessing of the day?*
> *What did you learn today?*
> *How can you move forward in faith tomorrow?*

A simple adaptation makes these questions meaningful for Bible study and prayerful reflection in the margins. Choose a text, read it, then begin to pray as you respond to these four questions:

> *What is the challenge of this text?*
> *What is the blessing of this text?*
> *What did you learn from this text?*
> *What can you take with you from this text to live more faithfully today and tomorrow?*

Consider trying these four questions with a text from the Psalms, or perhaps Isaiah 58, the Magnificat of Mary, or a passage from Romans.

Karen Weichman tells a story about a challenge she faced and an insight she gained:

What is the blessing of THIS day?

What is the challenge of this text?

I have Philippians 4:8, 9 underlined with "Uncle Buck's decision" in the margin. I remember this was when a girlfriend called and wanted to go to a movie, Sex, Lies, and Videotapes. *I had recently recommitted my life to the Lord and knew it was not something I wanted to watch. I told her I would call her back. After talking to another Christian friend about it and reading these verses, I got out the paper, found* Uncle Buck *was playing, and suggested we see it instead. She didn't understand, but we went to see* Uncle Buck. *I'll never forget this simple decision because the margin reminds me each time I see it on the page.*

Uncle
Buck
Decision

Ultimately, prayer creates new pathways. Prayer rewires the hardwiring of our hearts, minds, and souls. Praying in the margins creates new pathways for venturing forth into this life with wisdom and courage.

Praying for Home

Arthur R. Walls prayed to be home. In his Bible, next to Revelation 22, he wrote, *In my barracks at 10:40, Tuesday, June 4, 1918, I prayed to be home.* Perhaps his restraint teaches us as well. Choose a text. Name the time. Note the location. Jot down the date. Then write down the particular petition you most need at the time. In some way, any prayer we might write on the page is a variation of his. We are all praying to find our home in God, our true home, our true center. This was Arthur R. Walls's earnest prayer, and I think it is ours as well.

Praying in this inch of space, scrawling that line down the edge of the page, is at its most basic a prayer for finding our way home. That line is a pathway, not unlike two tin cans and a long string stretched between the bedrooms of siblings. The line stretches from us to God allowing us to name our deepest prayers and allowing God to nudge us on our way home.

Connecting with God

Mesu Andrews

For years, I used the margin in my Bible as my journal. And in the margin of my Bible, I struggled to come to terms with chronic illness.

Isaiah 38 tells about King Hezekiah's illness and subsequent healing. Illness changes us. Chronic illness changes us at the core of our beings. Hezekiah explains beautifully the transformation of character that occurs when we allow God to work through our suffering.

Isaiah 38:10, 14-16 (NIV):

> I said, "In the prime of my life
>   must I go through the gates of death
>   and be robbed of the rest of my years?"
> . . . .
> I cried like a swift or thrush,
>   I moaned like a mourning dove.
> My eyes grew weak as I looked to the heavens.
>   "I am being threatened; Lord, come to my aid!"
> But what can I say?
>   He has spoken to me, and he himself has
>   done this.
> I will walk humbly all my years
>   because of this anguish of my soul.
> Lord, by such things people live;
>   and my spirit finds life in them too.
> You restored me to health
>   and let me live.

The note in my margin says:

> Since the spring of 1996, I've experienced a litany of health problems. I have felt at times as though I will never be "myself" again. Honestly, I've forgotten who "myself" is. I wake up in the middle of the night with such discouragement and try to train my mind to praise the Lord, to present my requests to Him rather than worry. It helps to meditate on scripture, but my mind is so foggy, I can't concentrate. It helps to be completely transparent with you in prayer, Lord. At least I feel a little like "myself" when I do that. Perhaps "myself" isn't what I need to be. Perhaps You're creating a new me. Help me to embrace the character of that new creation I'm becoming, Lord.

Hezekiah was restored to health. I have not been . . . yet. Perhaps someday the Lord will heal me or medical science will discover cures for the various issues I endure. On good days, I celebrate the new "me" God is creating through these trials, and I thank Him for the deeper compassion, humility, and patience I'm learning. On the difficult days, I give myself grace and remember God's presence with me.

I have not yet been physically healed. Perhaps my healing comes in a different form.

On the Pages of Your Bible

- Choose one of the suggested "praying in that inch of space" practices. Find a favorite scripture and explore the text in a new way through this practice.

- Turn to 2 Timothy 3:12-17. What does Timothy affirm engagement with scripture will accomplish? Write down three elements necessary for creative reading of a holy text.

- Isaiah 38:10, prayed by Mesu Andrews, is a deep lament for the one who prays for healing. Use your margins to pray for your healing, others who are battling disease, and to pray for caregivers, doctors, nurses, and therapists.

- Betsy internalized the words of Romans 15:13 by drawing a creative interpretation of the words into her margin with colored pencils. Skim the memory verses below, choose one you appreciate and create a memorable picture in the margin to help you internalize the verse or verses.

Galatians 5:22-23	Matthew 16:26	Psalm 118:24
Isaiah 40:31	Philippians 4:13	Matthew 6:33
Proverbs 3:5-6	Psalm 37:4	Hebrews 13:1

- Choose a text that has troubled you or challenged you at some point in your life, and have a conversation with the text. Perhaps even use conversation bubbles in the style of a comic strip. God speaks from the left, you speak from the right. Draw a series of bubbles. Fill the bubbles with a conversation between you and God about the particular text.

- An often-neglected line in the famous "Serenity Prayer" asks that hardships become a pathway to peace. The prayer offers,

Living one day at a time,
Enjoying one moment at a time,
Accepting hardship as a pathway to peace.

Find a spot in your Bible to write and reflect on this portion of the Serenity Prayer. The original version and other variations may be found on the Internet for further exploration.

WRITING THROUGH CONFLICT

Whenever your heart speaks, take good notes.

—Judith Campbell

On the Edge

When we get out into the world—living those new horizons while praying vertically—we inevitably experience conflict. Our hearts cry out. 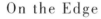We take notes to sort it all out.

Have you ever really felt pushed to the edge? You know—that place of conflict because of character or circumstance where you just feel crazy?

Mary Karr was on the edge.

Her mother was dying. Her own alcoholism was in remission. Even at this stage of life, with renewed health for herself and her mother's battle all too clear, the two of them could not get along.

By the end of the first evening of their visit, the two were scream-
ing at each other. By 3 a.m., Mary went out for a run to let off some
steam.

Upon arriving home, she pulled out her journal and turned to
the last page in which she had written. There were words from her
spiritual advisor, an oblate in the Catholic Church, with the encouragement to read six verses of Psalm 51.

Realizing she had left her Bible behind, she searched through
her mother's guest room in the middle of the night to find a Bible
to read. Deep in the drawer, she discovered her mother's childhood
Bible and turned to Psalm 51. Part of the psalm was circled in pale
blue crayon. As Mary describes the find, she makes clear that the
circled portion (verses 5-10) were the only verses assigned to her by
her spiritual director.

So she read:

> *Yes, I was born in guilt, in sin,*
>   *from the moment my mother conceived me.*
> *And yes, you want truth in the most hidden places;*
>   *you teach me wisdom in the most secret space.*
>
> *Purify me with hyssop and I will be clean:*
>   *wash me and I will be whiter than snow.*
> *Let me hear joy and celebration again;*
>   *let the bones you crushed rejoice once more.*
> *Hide your face from my sins;*
>   *wipe away all my guilty deeds!*
> *Create a clean heart for me, God;*
>   *put a new, faithful spirit deep inside me!*

But it was not until Mary turned to the second passage assigned
by her spiritual director that her heart started to pound. The journal
directed her to read James 1:12-15, and so she turned through her
mother's Bible, not seeing any other blue crayon wave lines, until she
arrived at the passage. And there it was, her mother's hand once again.

Those who stand firm during testing are blessed. They are tried and true. They will receive the life God has promised to those who love him as their reward. No one who is tested should say, "God is tempting me!" This is because God is not tempted by any form of evil, nor does he tempt anyone. Everyone is tempted by their own cravings; they are lured away and enticed by them. Once those cravings conceive, they give birth to sin; and when sin grows up, it gives birth to death.

As she flipped through all the pages of the Bible, Mary Karr came to realize that only two texts were marked in her mother's entire Bible, Psalm 51:5-10 and James 1:12-15. There is no explanation for the occurrence.

Mary describes the moment,

As miracles go, it may not even seem like one. But it feels as if God once guided my mother's small hand, circa 1920 something, to make two notes I'd very much need to find seventy years later—a message that I could be made new, that I am—have always been—loved.

Mock that experience as random chance if you like, but from then on, I started to arrive in the instant as never before, standing up in it as if pushed from behind like a wave, for it feels as if I was made—from all the possible shapes a human might take—not to prove myself worthy but to refine the worthy I'm formed from, acknowledge it, own it, spend it on others. . . . Every now and then we enter the presence of the numinous and deduce for an instant how we're formed, in what detail the force that infuses every petal might specifically run through us, wishing only to lure us into our full potential.

For Mary Karr, this was less providence and much more invitation. An invitation, delivered to her on the absolute edge, from the edges of scripture to be her very best self.

Sometimes, not one word needs to be penned in the margins of your Bible. Sometimes, a wavy line or a circle is all that is needed to call attention to the deep cracks in the conflicted places of the heart.

Conflict at the Margins

Life is marked by conflict. Some conflict is clear and on the surface demanding prayer, attention, and action. But so much more often, conflict is less conscious and more engrained—deeply tucked away in body and soul—begging to be named and brought out into the light. One of my seminary professors even ventured to say that conflict is where the work of the Holy Spirit begins.

Careful scripture reading allows us to name conflicts—in the text, in our understanding of God's nature, in our own experience. For Mary Karr, her conflict began with her own struggle with addiction and extended into the lifelong relationship with her mother. Going inward, and naming with all honesty, the conflict that is within us is where the work of the Holy Spirit can begin.

At some point, the words from James 1:12-15 had spoken to the heart of Mary Karr's mom. Who knew what conflict led her to this text? Who knows what revelation and change of heart she gleaned? And yet that chalky blue crayon circle speaks of conversion—something changed within when she read that text, back in the day, in 1920 something.

Christ, Solving Problems at the Margins

"Jesus bent down and wrote on the ground with his finger" (John 8:6).

We can't help but wonder why Jesus wrote. As the story of the

What DID Jesus write in the margin that day ??

woman about to be stoned unfolds in the Gospel of John, everything is escalating: the crowd, the tension, the accusations, and the emotion. Perhaps even the frustration of Jesus the Christ. In the midst of that tension, Jesus kneels down to write.

I love this image of the man in the sand. Here, on his knees with his finger in the dust he gains composure.

Jesus took that invitation to write when an angry crowd was ready to stone a woman who had committed adultery. In the Gospel of John, chapter 8, this text is so controversial many manuscripts did not include it. The story goes like this:

And Jesus went to the Mount of Olives. Early in the morning he returned to the temple. All the people gathered around him, and he sat down and taught them. The legal experts and Pharisees brought a woman caught in adultery. Placing her in the center of the group, they said to Jesus, "Teacher, this woman was caught in the act of committing adultery. In the Law, Moses commanded us to stone women like this. What do you say?" They said this to test him, because they wanted a reason to bring an accusation against him. Jesus bent down and wrote on the ground with his finger.

They continued to question him, so he stood up and replied, "Whoever hasn't sinned should throw the first stone." Bending down again, he wrote on the ground. Those who heard him went away, one by one, beginning with the elders. Finally, only Jesus and the woman were left in the middle of the crowd.

Jesus stood up and said to her, "Woman, where are they? Is there no one to condemn you?"

She said, "No one, sir."

Jesus said, "Neither do I condemn you. Go, and from now on, don't sin anymore."

One of the lingering mysteries in scripture is certainly that question: What did Jesus write?

Everyone has an idea. Perhaps the mystery is the beauty of the story because it lets our imagination come into play. But we can make some educated guesses.

Perhaps he doodled, letting his mind be drawn to a new place.

Perhaps he cross-referenced scripture, helping him to sort out the Law.

Perhaps he drew on a favorite text, guiding him to wisdom and love.

Perhaps he sketched a question mark.

Perhaps, he prayed for healing.

Perhaps, he went around the circle and named the sins of each person there.

Maybe, he took a deep breath.

Maybe, he looked to his Father for answers.

Some say, perhaps he wrote the Law, "Stone her" for the crowd to see while whispering to those gathered, "Whoever hasn't sinned should throw the first stone" (John 8:7).

Why did Jesus write? The text tells us he wrote a second time. Bending down again, he wrote on the ground (John 8:9). The mystery tugs at our curiosity and even our Christlike creativity.

Michael Card explored the text in his song, "Scribbling in the Sand." He sings how Jesus "shouted volumes" by scribbling in the sand. I wonder if we write, first and foremost, to find our voice. With that clarity, we move from silence to a speech shaped by text and script that has a divine volume in a noisy world.

Card prays that same finger might come to create "unexpected space" in his own heart, mind, and soul. Could the Jesus who doodles in the sand, who writes into the margins of the law, come and do some writing in our own souls? In that unexpected space, the margins, we come to understand this Jesus who scribbles in the sand and sketches into our souls new words and new life. For Card, we write to craft that unexpected space.

Jesus took the chaos at hand, and with a stroke in the sand, created a blank slate. The creative answer to the problem was as simple as a scribble in the dust of the earth. In the conversation with the Pharisees, the text of judgment stands bold. It was in the presence of the margins, and a new stroke there, that new life emerged. A golden canon, a divine proportion transformed the ratio of judgment to grace.

With a stroke of his finger at the edge of this controversy, by writing in the sand, Jesus changed the script of this story. And that is how writing in the margins can be in the lives of Christians. Writing in the margins is a spiritual practice that can change the text of our own spiritual stories. In my own life, writing in the margins has sometimes transformed a grumble into a plea for help, or a bout of malaise into a small praise for the small goodness that came even in the midst of a dark day.

What Jesus does here, by writing in the margins, is solve a problem. Perhaps so, too, can we.

Margin of Safety

At our edge, we find God's pledge—that promise to provide, provoke, and protect.

Consider the very phrases where we use the word *margin*: a margin of safety, margin of error, we'll meet at the margin.

Something happens in this place that moves us from our edges to God's pledge to bless.

The beauty of the margin is that in that ring around the edges of your Bible there is an inherent circle of blessing. The content that the circle holds—scripture—is the greatest gift we will ever receive. The circle itself is a safe space, a sanctuary of sorts, for working out the conflicts of our inner life, our faith development, and our broken world. This might just be the place where some of our deepest conflicts are worked out and solved.

This circle is a place that calls us to worship. Here, confessions are named, offerings presented, discernment revealed, and invocations uttered. Lives are changed in this circle in ways big and small. Mary Karr is just one example of someone who experienced that blessing as she confessed the stuff of her heart and was met with a grace that superseded all of her expectations.

Freed for New Life

As we work out those conflicts—like Mary Karr, even like Jesus—we find new freedom for ourselves and for those we love. They met conflict in prayer and patience. They waited and wrote. They looked for creative guidance and then found themselves writing their way into new answers.

There is an old adage that says, "Dirty Bible, Clean Heart." Another variation of the same theme attributed to Charles Spurgeon offers, "A Bible that's falling apart usually belongs to someone who isn't." Every marginal note in some way is a variation on the theme Mary Karr's spiritual guide pressed into her hand with Psalm 51:10, "Create a clean heart for me, God; / put a new, faithful spirit deep inside me!"

So in some strange way, messing up our Bibles means freeing up our hearts and minds from the clutter that constrains and conflicts us.

Connecting with God

Dennis Malachow

Some years ago at a crossroads in my life, I found myself in a Texas jail. Born and raised in Pittsburgh, Pennsylvania, married to my high school sweetheart, two beautiful kids, a great job, surrounded by loving family and friends—but none of it mattered to me. I had a heart in love with sin. I drove off leaving everything and everyone I had ever known behind. Alcohol, drugs, and selfishness had led me to walk away from everything I had known and loved. As a kid I grew up in church and my belief in God's existence and presence were never in doubt; yet a different force led me. Things were about to change.

Over the next several years and through twelve states, I blew through relationships, jails, prisons, and homelessness. I found myself, along with twenty other men, in a space the size of an average living room of a middle-class American home. Half of them did not speak English, and the other half were gang members. This left a lot of time for reading and thinking. The Bible became my source of strength. I spent six months in this room. Over this period of time, God in his grace and mercy, poured his love into my heart.

One night in jail, God brought to my memory how my grandmother would have me sit on her lap as a child as she would talk to God. She would speak to God out loud. I knew this was real. Her lip would quiver and tears would fill her eyes as she prayed. This was a daily event when I was with her. It was now twenty-five years later and God had eliminated the gap of time as I was reading Psalm 23.

As I read the psalm, I realized my grandmother, who was once surrounded by so many loved ones and friends, was now alone. Her husband and son (my father) had passed away. Her brothers and sisters had either passed away or moved away. She now lived in a senior high-rise alone. This night, as I was reading Psalm 23, we became united once again. Twenty-five years and two thousand miles melted away.

In my Bible, over the words "my," "I," and "me," I wrote "our," "we," and "us." I would now pray the psalm like this, "The Lord is OUR shepherd, WE shall not want. He makes US to lie down in green pastures." Each day the presence of God would always comfort me as I prayed the psalm this way. Since then, God has continued to guide and comfort me. I now live an hour away from my grandmother. We discuss God often and pray together at times. It has been thirty years since I sat on her lap praying to God. Now we sit together knowing the Lord is OUR shepherd.

On the Pages of Your Bible

- Galatians 5:1 speaks to our freedom in Christ. Take your Bible to a place where you can engage the news of the world (television, computer, newspaper). Write a prayer for freedom for those in particular places in our world where violence and oppression reign.

- While you have access to world news, find an image—a face—of someone far across the world. Look at the shape and color of their eyes, the turn of their smile, and notice their other unique features. Now, turn in your Bible to the priestly benediction in Numbers 6:24-26 and write a prayer for the Lord's blessing and keeping of the stranger whose photo you engaged.

- Psalm 51:10 prays for a clean heart. The old adage says, "Dirty Bible, Clean Heart." Put some of your life dirt on the Bible page and offer these words to God as a confession.

- Read Romans 3:10–8:39. Consider this a series of "stepping stones." Write in your margins—as steps—the key pieces of information that shape your journey to Christ.

- Writing in the sand helped Jesus gain his composure in John 8. Read the story in your Bible. Write in the margin one thing to remember from the text, one thing to wonder about the text, and one thing to live into action from the text.

PRACTICING SCRIPTURAL DISCIPLINES

The Bible is alive, it speaks to me; it has feet, it runs after me;
it has hands, it lays hold of me.

—Martin Luther

Scripture is at the heart of margin writing.

Scripture is the first stroke on the sacred page. In the margins surrounding that text we have an opportunity to wrestle with the text, take notes of our context, and be in conversation with God about the sinful subtext of our lives. Questions, knowledge, insights, confession, thanksgivings, challenges, key words, revelations, calls to worship, calls to action, and prayers sparked by scripture, all of these are the writings of a scriptural practice. Scripture prompts, probes, pushes, and propels us to engage. That engagement happens sometimes in silence and in stillness, but it is realized and internalized by scribbling on the page the revelations that break through.

Weekly, and sometimes daily, marginal musing often feeds my soul. I feel calmer with pen in hand. I need engagement with a story other than my own. I need inspiration through the metaphors and meaning of scripture. I need a revolution from this technological age toward an intimacy between myself, the page and a pencil in hand. I need insight and transformation into my patterns of emotional reaction. I need patience. I need help in decision making. I need help in remembering. I need a salvation story greater than the latest ad on television. And those are just *my* needs. The list multiplies exponentially as we add the prayerful needs of the world.

Something about having pen in hand and a blank column down the side of the page allows something deep and wonderful to happen. No mountaintops are needed. Simply climbing above self and standing on scripture to gain insight into the vast and beautiful world of God's creation lifts my spirit and draws me outside of myself.

Often in the church we talk of "spiritual disciplines." I like to think of margin musing as *scriptural* discipline. Certainly we have a life of prayer. Certainly we cultivate practices of heart and mind that create a space for God. Certainly those disciplines of spirit are necessary. But in an age where so much of our population is biblically illiterate, perhaps the first and foremost discipline that is taught is this scriptural discipline. Read the sacred text, pick up pen in hand, and see what happens as that script intersects the script of your own life and the world around you. In a world where "user interface" is all too often screen time, writing in the margins offers a transformed interaction where we encounter God face-to-face through the words on the page. Perhaps a move from spiritual disciplines to scriptural discipline will help get us deeper in the text. The invitation to a different practice, of scriptural work, is intended so that word becomes work, scripture becomes service, prose becomes practice.

Disciplines That Connect the Generations

Adam Copeland, a young adult of this generation, speaks to that kind of transformed user interface when he talks about writing in the pages of his Bible,

I write in my Bible's margins during meaningful points in my faith journey. In high school, when a close friend of mine died, I marked-up the psalm read at her funeral. As I struggled to decide where to attend college, I reflected in the margins on a passage that helped me gain clarity on the school with the best fit. Later, when I studied abroad during college, I marked Psalm 29 after it was read at a sunrise service on an Egyptian beach. The margins of Ephesians 4 include a note reminding me it was read when I was elected to a position of national church leadership more than ten years ago. In 2006, I marked the first passage I studied during my introductory preaching class in seminary. My Bible's margins are marked with dozens of dates and connections, signposts on my journey.

I once read my Bible straight through from Genesis to Revelation (it took more than a year). When I did so, I always had a red colored pencil nearby to mark passages and comment on them in the margins. Though every book of my Bible has red underlines somewhere, it's the other markings that are more meaningful because they correspond to particular dates, experiences, and memories.

The Bible tells the story of God's people—and God's steadfast love for them—from the beginning of creation until now. My Bible, with its scribbled notes marking my journey, is a reminder that God is present and active in my life as well. The marks tell me that my story is connected, ultimately, to God's story.

"The marks tell me that my story is connected." Adam is almost revolutionary in these reflections in allowing a new kind of connection amid our overconnected, and all too falsely connected, digital age. "My story is connected, ultimately, to God's story." Adam's scriptural disciplines have made a mark on his life and called that life into a greater story.

If anything, when we consider the margins, God's patience is that we too often have placed God in the margins of our lives. God waits with patience, grace, and love for that alignment to be renegotiated. Ironically, when we enter the margins of the Bible, God becomes first and foremost in our hearts and minds. It is our life that is meant to be marginal as we hold God's word central in all things. God's patience is that God has been marginal in our lives. We try and assert our narratives, our disciplines, and our own texts into the world instead of letting God's narrative be central.

Drawing God Out from the Margins

I am fascinated by the margin writing of an Australian named Phil Pringle. Each day on his blog he posts a marginal note on a few verses of scripture. The image appears as a large black rectangle. In the top left of the image, the verse from scripture is printed in white. Across the remainder of the rectangle, emerging from the words of the scripture text, is the scrawl of his hand in prayer. In yellows, pinks, greens, purple, and white he writes notes and prayers and revelation from the scripture text upon which he has been meditating. On October 1, 2012, he reflected on Psalm 1:1-3. The psalm reflects on the one who is rooted in the Word of God, planted there like a tree by streams of water. Phil adds to the text:

There is as much blessing in what you don't do as in what you do.
Choose your environment, associates, and friends with wisdom.

[The psalmist] loves the word of God—sign of spiritual health—appetite for the Bible. What fills your thoughts all day and night? Make your mind think on, chew the word of God. It will break open with light. The life of the Word within makes you fruitful, healing, planted by refreshing influences. The BIG promise here is that whatever you do will prosper!!! Start meditating in the Word TODAY!

The words above only barely convey the energy, joy, and creativity he finds on the page. The words burst with a keen sense of what the scripture might mean if integrated into our lives with gusto. The passion of his script seems to me a prayer that we all might be drawn by his scriptural disciplines into our own. He understands, just like my husband Jason, how we all too often marginalize God—our maker, creator, and redeemer. Our scriptural disciplines draw God back into the forefront of our lives, our prayers, our every action. Scriptural disciplines shape us.

Once we are shaped, even this broken world, might be shaped by our renewed commitment to live out the Kingdom as scripture calls us to do.

What I have seen through my own margin writing is a clear call to love and serve those on the margins of society.

PSALM 1:1-3
...Start meditating on the Word today!

Connecting with God

Jonathan Ammon

The practice of placing notes next to the text forces me to interrogate every verse. What does this mean? Do I understand this? How do the writers make their argument? What is their argument? I find that this significantly slows down my reading but gives me an opportunity to inquire of God over many portions of scripture that I let slide past my attention before.

Margin notes are my personal and often intimate responses to the voice of the Lord in scripture. I write in the margins prayers to God and engage the scripture as dialogue spoken directly to me. They include confessions of sin, confessions of faith, supplications and petitions, thanksgivings and praises. In addition, I added a practice of a dear friend and mentor who dates each note so that in years to come each revelation has a tag to show God's faithfulness and my own maturing process over time. These notes create an "Ebenezer" that documents the promise and voice of the Holy Spirit.

Then Samuel took a stone and set it up between Mizpah and Jeshanah. He named it Ebenezer, explaining, "The LORD helped us to this very point." (1 Samuel 7:12)

On the Pages of Your Bible

- Check out the blog of Phil Pringle. Try his style of scriptural discipline: writing in the margin of your Bible, freehand, with boldness, joy, and urgency. Pay attention to your emotions as you write. What does this practice free you to do and pray?

- Jonathan Ammon speaks of his "Ebenezer"—a stone of help—from 1 Samuel 7:12. Read this text in its context. What are your "Ebenezers"? Write these in gratitude in your margin.

- Romans 12:1-2 offers insight into transformed lives. Reflect on this text in your margin. What needs to change in your life to live into this message?

- As Romans 12 continues, in verses 9-18 we read a litany of specific practices that are shaped by scripture. In your margins, choose one you want to practice. Write in your margin a specific place where you might live out this scriptural discipline

- In the margin next to 2 Timothy 3:16 write your reflections on the purpose of scripture in your life and for your life in this world.

LIVING IN THE MARGINS

Love and trust and justice, concern for the poor,
that's being pushed to the margins, and you can see it.

—*Cornel West*

The most hearty of margin writers are those who ink into the middle margins, the ones tucked into the cracks and pressed into the spine of the Bible. This seemingly unreachable place becomes a prayer for the ultimate outcome of writing in the margins, that is, living in the margins.

This particular place, in the field of typography, is called "the gutter."

Writing in the cracks — "the gutter."

Our lives are meant to be marginal. The text of the Bible is intended to push us and prod us into the margins. The word of God pierces, and then pushes us out of our comfort zone into the places of discomfort and the hearts of the discomforted.

We do not write in the margins just for ourselves. We write in the margins to gain strength for sharing faith, hope and love, justice,

For sharing:
Faith Justice
Hope Mercy
Love Kindness

mercy, and kindness with others who ache for just that. The margins are meant to nudge us to the poor and oppressed, the widowed and the orphaned, the ones who are imprisoned by bars or addiction. This is where the margins work on us. And perhaps it is just those inner margins, those that fall into the cracks, that remind us of all the people in this world who do fall into the cracks.

I cannot read Isaiah 58 without beginning to pray for those in the margins. Verse 12 describes the unlivable streets, the broken walls, the ruins and the broken foundations. Next to Isaiah 58 in my Bible during seminary I wrote after hearing a friend's sermon: "Am I willing to step into the cracks?"

> *If you open your heart to the hungry,*
> *and provide abundantly for those who are afflicted,*
> *your light will shine in the darkness,*
> *and your gloom will be like the noon.*
> *The Lord will guide you continually*
> *and provide for you, even in parched places.*
> *He will rescue your bones.*
> *You will be like a watered garden,*
> *like a spring of water that won't run dry.*
> *They will rebuild ancient ruins on your account;*
> *the foundations of generations past you will restore.*
> *You will be called*
> *Mender of Broken Walls,*
> *Restorer of Livable Streets.*
>
>   (Isaiah 58:10-12)

The opening of hearts begins in the margin and continues out into those cracked and crevassed streets. The promise of Isaiah 58 for those willing to venture forth is that the Lord will "guide you continually and provide for you." By your work and the power of God, broken walls will be mended and unlivable streets restored. The margins of this world need our work and God's word.

*praying for those in the margins : ISAIAH 58:10-12

Is it possible that our Bible's margins might nudge us out the door into the margins of this world to offer just what Cornell West suggests: concern for the poor, trust and justice, and love?

Concern for the Poor in the Margins

The words we write into our margins—filling our margins with commentary, word studies, cross-references, and thematic associations—shapes us and calls us into new ways of living. Marginal practices are just what the writer of Leviticus wanted us to understand of God's command in Leviticus 23. The margins matter—in the way we plan our weeks, plant our fields, and find rest in our days. The margins matter, in the way we connect to God on the edge of the page in our personal Bibles. Each informs the other. Most important, these marginal practices matter for the ways we do justice, love kindness, and walk humbly with God as we interact with those who cross our path each day.

Gregory Boyle, author of *Tattoos on the Heart: The Power of Boundless Compassion*, invites us to move from "gutter" mentality to consider the wide circle of God's compassion. His words are a powerful call for transformation:

No daylight to separate us. Only kinship. Inching ourselves closer to creating a community of kinship such that God might recognize it. Soon we imagine, with God, this circle of compassion. Then we imagine no one standing outside of that circle, moving ourselves closer to the margins so that the margins themselves will be erased. We stand there with those whose dignity has been denied. We locate ourselves with the poor and the powerless and the voiceless. At the edges, we join the easily despised and the readily left out. We stand with the demonized so that the demonizing will stop. We situate ourselves right next to the disposable so that the day will come when we stop throwing people away.

Dwelling in the margins of scripture, particularly the gutter in the middle, compels us to live marginally in our everyday lives.

Founder of Homeboy Industries in Los Angeles and former pastor of the Dolores Mission Church, Boyle is a Jesuit priest with great concern for the poor and impoverished. His ministry has stretched from the margins of Bolivia, to the hallways of a prison complex, to the backstreets of the barrios in Los Angeles.

I wish I had access to Gregory Boyle's Bible. I have no doubt it's filled with gut-wrenching prayers and life-giving moments of hope. What I do have are a few of his thoughts, spelled out in his incredible book, about where he gets his conviction regarding his concern for the poor:

> *Not much in my life makes any sense outside of God. Certainly, a place like Homeboy Industries is all folly and bad business unless the core of the endeavor seeks to imitate the kind of God one ought to believe in. In the end, I am helpless to explain why anyone would accompany those on the margins were it not for some anchored belief that the Ground of all Being thought this was a good idea.*

Trust and Justice in the Margins

If Boyle is a modern-day saint, I want to make sure you meet Mary Slessor—a saint from another day. Born in Scotland, during the nineteenth century, her alcoholic father wreaked havoc on her life and the life of her family. He was financially irresponsible and physically abusive. Mary and her siblings worked from a very young age in the local cotton mill to ensure they had food to eat.

Taking her inspiration from David Livingston, Mary moved to

Gut-wrenching prayers · Life-giving moments of HOPE

Calabar (modern-day Nigeria) at age twenty-seven, after the death of her father. Mary became a mother there to many orphans. Even more so, she found herself welcoming all of the twins born in the community. At this time, bearing twins was considered an evil curse. She took them all in. Isn't that what truth and justice does in the margins?

Now, in several locations across Nigeria, there are statues of Mary Slessor carrying a child in each arm—twins—whole and happy, having survived thanks to Slessor's belief in truth and justice.

Mary also championed the rights of women in the African communities in which she lived. In her Bible, we can see a bit of her feisty spirit, of her concern for other women, and of her bold willingness to venture, as an unmarried woman, to remote missionary fields: there next to Ephesians 5:24, where Paul encourages the women of Ephesus to "submit to their husbands," Mary has written "Nay, nay, Paul laddie. This will na do."

" Nay, nay,
Paul Laddie.
This will na do. "

Because of her own upbringing, Mary knew the fear and domination of unjust systems. She knew what distrust and injustice could do to a wife, to a child, to a family. Through her work in Africa, she saw that distrust and injustice play out on a societal scale. "Nay, nay," we can now see her saying, "This will na do."

Living Love in the Margins

Of all the amazing margins I have encountered, the margins that have had the most lasting impact may be those of McKenzie Noelle Wilson. Just fifteen, the margins of her Bible are a living witness to her growing faith. In her margins, one can see her faith coming to life. Growing up in Jacksonville, Florida, McKenzie loved cheerleading and softball. Her vivacious personality encouraged friends and strangers. For one of her teenage birthday parties, she asked friends to bring money, instead of gifts, that would be donated to an orphanage.

On August 17, 2010, McKenzie died suddenly due to a rare inflammation of her brain. Her family and friends grieved. More than 1,800 people attended her funeral. What she left behind, a legacy of kindness and generosity, had its foundation in the margins of her Bible, where she wrote:

I found a love
nothing can compare
I belong to you but I'm afraid to lose my friends.

Her father shared the Bible with Ben Williams, a member of the band Eleven22 from the Beach United Methodist Church in Jacksonville. The margins, filled with McKenzie's prayers, inspired Ben and his band to develop an entire album to share her story with others.

"The Reason" is filled with songs sung from her pages. Proceeds from the album benefit the building of orphanages in Uganda. From those sales, several homes have been built—a home for orphaned boys, a home for orphaned girls, and a home for abandoned babies. And then, months after the album came out, the McKenzie Noelle Wilson Foundation was founded, which offers service to those in the margins of Jacksonville through local efforts and continues the work of Eleven22 in Uganda. Among other things, the foundation has built, in Lugandan, Amaka ga McKenzie, or "McKenzie's Home," an orphanage that feeds, educates, and generally nurtures twenty young girls who would otherwise have nothing. Across the bright blue walls of the home, painted butterflies abound. The building stands out in brilliant contrast to the otherwise stark surroundings.

McKenzie prayed in her margins that she would not lose her friends. Now, through her foundation, her friends are growing in their leadership and new friends are being made in her name in the communities of Jacksonville, Florida, and Uganda.

What happens in the margins of the page is that we realize how God has picked us up and out of the margins. We are saved and

God's PICKING US UP from the margins IS PRECISELY the thing that allows us to DWELL with, LEARN from, & SERVE those on the margins of our society.

graced and blessed and loved, in spite of everything. *I belong to you,* McKenzie wrote. We find our belonging to the One who believes in us. When we find that belief, we can then share that belonging with others. We can then tell those who are lost that we believe in them. God's picking us up from the margins is precisely the thing that allows us to dwell with, learn from, and serve those on the margins of our society.

Being Pushed to the Margin

In nature, when two different kind of ecosystems meet, something amazing happens. It is at the margin of two opposing landscapes where the world is most alive and the flora and the fauna are most varied. Here is where life thrives. For us, living into the margins can be discomforting and painful because we are pushed out of our comfort zones.

Maybe it's just the reason that the very word *margin* holds within itself a contradiction of sorts. Margin can mean a comfort, an allowance, even, a cushion. Here there is room to breathe, a place to fall, a safety net in which to fall. But margin also has another sense— brink, rim, and edge are all connotations of the word *margin*. In that sense, we are breathless, about to fall, and not certain of any safety net.

The margins of the Bible hold that tension. We find comfort and rim, allowance and edge, cushion and brink on the edge of the page. When we navigate the crevice where those two meet, with the full assurance that the Lord is *my God and my all,* we find strength and insight for all the other breaks and cracks and valleys of this world.

This is precisely the place where the Lord will guide those who live in the margins continually, rescuing our tired bones and providing water in the parched places.

Close to the equator, in Masaka, Uganda, where one of the great economic activities is gathering grasshoppers, several ecosystems merge. The River Nabajuzi and the Kumbu Forest fall within a short distance of Lake Victoria and the Victoria Falls. This is where Amaka ga McKenzie stands as testament to the promise of Isaiah 58.

Love, trust, justice, and concern for the poor: Are we willing to get pushed to the margins? If, like McKenzie, we are willing to go, God will continue to meet us there.

ARE WE WILLING TO GET PUSHED TO THE Margins?

Connecting with God

Kathy Snider

I did not plant the chili bush outside my front door squeezed right next to the cement edge of the patio. It appeared on its own—like grace—undeserved favor. I love chilis like a good Mexican would—the green serranos of my bush made into salsa I use on almost everything I eat. I always say my nine months in Mexico before my Guatemala life gifted me with a love for Our Lady of Guadalupe and a love for hot chilies—the Jalapeño version.

So now, here in Guatemala, thanks to my chili bush, I have a constant supply of small green serrano peppers I gather each morning for an added kick to the daily beans and eggs or to share with my neighbors.

One day however, Maria, my knowing neighbor, commented, "Your chili plant is drying up. Look at the leaves turning yellow. And there is less fruit now. It's going to die." She was right, I thought. My heart and taste buds dropped.

A few days later however, Teresa, my friend and household helper informed, "*Ojala corte una rama y la planta va a producir mas*—hopefully you'll cut off a branch and the plant will produce more." "Really?" I said. "Let's do it." So Teresa grabbed the machete and expertly whacked off a prominent branch of the chili plant. And that was that.

Shortly thereafter, I left for a trip to Coban and Antigua for rest and for business. I returned two weeks later greeted by my chili bush LOADED with peppers—green and plump just like a Christmas tree all adorned with lights. Wow! And then I remembered a line in the margins of my Bible from the Gospel of John chapter 15:2, "He removes every branch in me that bears no fruit. *Every branch that bears fruit he prunes to make it bear more fruit*" (NRSV, emphasis added).

As ruthless as it seems, I'm told pruning is essential. It's a way of making sure the plant's growing power is directed to producing more fruit instead of just longer branches. It is the "necessary pain" that produces growth. It is nature's theology of suffering, I think. So when the whacking begins in my own life, I keep a long and steady gaze on my chili bush laden with green peppers and note in particular the place where the severed branch had been.

That's it. I'm trusting that the suffering in my own hurting, broken, and at times messy life is transformed into the fruits I'm most in need of—like love, joy, peace, patience, kindness, and long-suffering—qualities I'm not able to produce on my own. I need the Master Pruner's touch. The cutting hurts but the benefits outweigh the pain. So speaks my chili plant and the Gospel of John.

When a part of me is being pruned—be it stress in relationships, illness, or loss of a loved one—my eyes are on a chili bush outside my front door with fruit waiting to be picked. Those make great salsa after all.

On the Pages of Your Bible

- Cornel West speaks prophetically when he names what is being pushed to the margin in the world today. Read Amos 5:21-24. What does the Lord God hate in the world of Amos? What does God hope for from the world today? Write responses to these in your margin. Then, consider our world today. What would be the parallel for what God might hate, and for what God might hope?

- Isaiah 58:1-9a concludes with a powerful affirmation that God will say, "Here I am" to the individual who cries to God for help. Use note-taking in the text to make note of the flow of this verse. Circle the questions asked. How do these questions lead to the three "thens" in verses 7-9? How do the questions and affirmations work together to move the reader to the culmination of verse 9a?

- Isaiah 58:9b-14 describes a changed world that will emerge. Write in the margin what actions we need to do to live into that change. Write in the margin what actions God will do. Draw a picture, using the imagery of Isaiah 58:12 to depict this changed world.

> *If you remove the yoke from among you,*
> *the finger-pointing, the wicked speech;*
> *if you open your heart to the hungry,*
> *and provide abundantly for those who are afflicted,*
> *your light will shine in the darkness,*
> *and your gloom will be like the noon.*
> *The LORD will guide you continually*
> *and provide for you, even in parched places.*
> *He will rescue your bones.*
> *You will be like a watered garden,*

like a spring of water that won't run dry.
They will rebuild ancient ruins on your account;
*   the foundations of generations past you will restore.*
You will be called
*   Mender of Broken Walls,*
*   Restorer of Livable Streets.*

(Isaiah 58:9b-12)

MARGINAL WRITING
IN A DIGITAL AGE

Annotation covers a broad territory.
It has been construed in many ways: as link making, as path building,
as commentary, as marking in or around existing text,
as a decentering of authority, as a record of reading
and interpretation, or as community memory.

—*Catherine C. Marshall*

With a simple tag of "#LASTPRINTISSUE," seventy-nine years of weekly news publishing changed as *Newsweek* distributed the last print issue of their magazine. The issue marks a milestone of changes. The time in which we receive news has shrunk from weekly information to momentary updates. The process by which news is reported is less a group effort and now more citizen journalism. Most dramatic, of course, is the material itself. Gone are the days when we leaf through the pages of a magazine.

Now, we scroll down a screen and stroke our finger to turn the page to a new digital image. What does this mean for the future of biblical margin writing?

One could easily answer, "everything." The silky vellum of the page is a thing of the past. Even more so, the pen. For those who love that feel of pen pressed to palm and the fluid capacity of the perfect pen to glide across the page, the digital age brings a certain kind of grief. But margin writing is not only about the pen and paper. It is more centrally about link-making, path-building, commentary, and memory.

In worship, I regularly sit behind a college student named Sarah Carlson. I have to tease her some days that her mom often sends her a text during church. One day after a sermon, I saw her scrolling through her cell phone. She quickly whispered, "I'm not texting!" Then she showed me the "Bible 360" app for her iPhone that allows her to take margin notes next to the biblical text. She had been "writing in the margins" all through worship. I loved seeing her excitement. She was drawing new paths and creating new links.

Making Our Marks

Catherine C. Marshall, a Silicon Valley expert in the annotation of texts in a digital age, has been my tutor in electronic annotation. Marshall argues that annotation is nothing more and nothing less than a record of reading and interpretation. Annotation marks a process of reception, internalization, processing, and claim-making. Annotation animates the text, which then animates our lives. Annotation is not dependent upon the page, but upon a process.

So margin writing is possible in everything from ebooks for the Nook as well as iBooks for the iPad. What matters, some will suggest, is that the book has made a mark. We have been changed by our engagement with the characters on the screen and the story

NOTE TO SELF:
check out BIBLE 360 APP

those characters tell. We mark what makes us stop and think. The words then, mark us, and make us live and move and have our very being in new and different ways.

Some will even argue the increasing value of a Bible marked in the margins on a digital page. Annotations become "searchable" so we can find the notes we make to ourselves as if they were filed away in a digital drawer. We can search for "popular highlights" where others have found a text that is important, made a note, and offered those insights to share. What has been intensely personal and private in the past is now sharable through public forums.

At this point, I must confess that I am a fan of pen and paper. My husband tells me I'm more centered when I've been about those marginal practices of writing, doodling, praying, and seeking. So I keep at it, as best I can, using my favorite pen and my Bible.

Still, I am intrigued by the work of Catherine C. Marshall and her thoughts about annotations in a digital age. What she makes us consider is what matters most in those margins. She comes up with quite a list that makes us think about what happens with those marks in the margins, for they are:

- Markers of interpretive activity
- Signals of procedures in reading
- Tools for problem-solving
- Visible traces of the reader's attention
- Incidental notes of reflection
- Place-markers and memory aids

Her research makes me look at my margins in new ways. And I wonder if her research really serves as important foundation in a time where everything seems to be changing more and more quickly. The last edition of *Newsweek* is just the first of many changes yet to come. What Marshall helps us to remember is how reading and annotating shapes us, marks us, molds us, and motivates us to learn and live anew. So we get back into scripture, whether on page or on a screen, looking for guidance.

- MARKERS OF INTERACTIVE ACTIVITY
- SIGNALS of PROCEDURES IN READING
- TOOLS for PROBLEM-SOLVING
- VISIBLE TRACES OF THE READER'S ATTENTION
- INCIDENTAL NOTES of REFLECTION
- PLACE-MARKERS & MEMORY AIDS.

Seeking the Transcendent

It is precisely because so much *has* changed, in this day and age, that we need that sacred text. When lulled by the trance of the screen, all the more do we need that transcendent dimension in our lives. When we are beguiled by our ability to "shape worlds" through gaming or voting online, all the more do we need a deeper understanding of the story that reveals God at work shaping our world and our lives.

In our world that has all too much stuff, we might simplify by focusing on soul and substance. Hearts. Voices. The text of the Bible. When soul and substance come together, so much is revealed. Patterns of meaning-making in an all-too-complicated world. Personal involvement with texts that nurture faith, hope, and love. Prayer life that is vital—finding its roots in scripture and its growth in living. Purposeful living that finds its origins in scripture. Particular verses highlighted that form a life's vision and mission. This is what marginalia means to us. These are incredible legacies. They contain the greatest hope and deepest pulse of life. When they are inked onto the page, their veins enliven us to engage the world where we may be lost in wonder, love, and praise. When they are typed onto the screen, those pixels help us see new pictures as our imaginations are enlivened.

A Luminous Life

As I prayed and thought about annotating texts in a digital age, a strange image kept coming to mind. I kept thinking about an artist, Makoto Fujimura, who created illustrations to illuminate portions of the Bible for the twenty-first century in honor of the four-hundreth anniversary of the King James Bible.

His medium is neither page and pen, nor mouse and screen.

Handwritten margin note:
* incredible legacies
* GREATEST HOPE
* DEEPEST PULSE of life

Instead, when he works in his studio he opens his Bible, sets a large canvas next to the margin, and then lies down upon a rolling plywood bed that allows free movement around and across the large studio floor. The canvas becomes, for him, an extension of the margins. He uses an ancient Japanese art practice called *Nihonga* to bring the text to life through this abstract art form.

The canvasses that emerge from this process are reminiscent of Rothko, and perhaps even Marc Chagall who simply had to illustrate scripture. The Bible reshaped what Chagall saw in the world and he had to create art to shape us to see some sense of what he saw. Makoto's paintings are expansive and yet restrained, they speak deeply specifics of a sacred story and yet they are abstract. The images sparkle with a sense of the transcendent; they are truly illuminations. Gold leaf dances across the screen. Light is evoked even from the darkest of places.

Through his artwork, Makoto is a margin-writer. The canvas is an extension of his margins; the two literally border each other as the process begins. The words of scripture mark him, change him, and in a way overflow from within in so much that they must spill out, they seep out through his veins and through his brushes onto the canvas. The margins of his Bible are too small to receive all this. The canvas catches the overflow. As I watch him work, I wonder what it would look like for me to move through the studios of my life nudging the margin of my Bible up against everything I engage each day in work and in play.

One of his paintings, "Golden Fire," stands as hinge between the era of the page and the onset of the screen. The wall-sized image looks like an open book complete with center spine, script, and small margins around the text. But the book blurs through the ebb and flow of predominantly gold leaf to look more akin to a golden screen. Made of mineral pigments and gold leaf on *kumohada* paper, the painting is an exquisite testament to this day and age. We are in between page and screen. But that discussion recedes into what stands alone as true: this text is transcendent. The luminosity within it cannot be held back by any medium. Instead, what emerges is sacred and aglow. His is truly an illuminated manuscript for this century and this luminosity will stand the test of time.

Just as Catherine C. Marshall makes us consider the essence of margin writing in a digital age, Makoto helps us see that essence as well. Both of them help us discover the broad territory that annotation allows. The Bible speaks of *so great* a reality, there is so much in this text, that it always overflows and demands more room, more space, more of, well, us. So that we ourselves might become luminous.

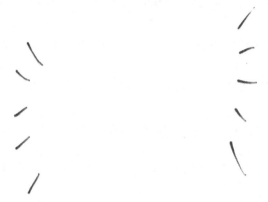

Connecting with God

Jimmy Tate

Personalizing the word is the way I live out the application of the word.

I will write a note then date it as well. These remind me later of the moment the Spirit of God reiterated that truth to my heart with vigor!

For example: I was ministering for a week at Auburn University. I was to speak on campus, and in area churches, as well. I did not FEEL like ministering, speaking, or doing anything for God that week; I was in a spiritual wilderness.

My regular Bible reading found me in the book of Acts. Philip was in Samaria. (As I was ministering in a faraway town, so was Philip.)

I read with little or no emotional connection, whatsoever.

And then I read Acts 8:13 (NASB), "Even Simon himself believed; and after being baptized, he continued on with Philip, and as he observed signs and great miracles taking place, *he was constantly amazed*" (emphasis added).

That phrase leapt off the page and landed in my heart.

I prayed upon reading that and asked for that experience that day on campus at Auburn to be burned in my heart.

God amazed me that day with incredible, miraculous sovereign appointments with students in dire need of Jesus.

That night, back at home, I opened my Bible—you guessed it, to Acts 8; verse 13 is underlined and highlighted with a bold asterisk. Sometime before that day, this verse mattered so much I gave it a star. Today, if you were to see page 1042 in my Bible, you would see added next to that star: April, 1998 @ Auburn, AL.

I know what that notation means—be amazed always.

I remember what great things God did that day. And, it continues to build my faith, presently, and into the ongoing adventure with Jesus.

There are other places in my Bible that are dated, highlighted to remind myself of what God spoke to me. Experiences in London, Budapest, Haiti, for instance, are ever with me, still. Why? Because they are not only in my past, but are also in my present, as they are marked and visible even now.

And because they are marked, I am marked as well. I am a marked man.

On the Pages of Your Bible

- Zechariah 8 shares a vision for a new day and age in Jerusalem when the streets will be restored after a time of exile. Read that vision with Catherine C. Marshall's quotation in hand. How does her quotation illumine this text for you?

  > Annotation covers a broad territory. It has been construed in many ways: as link making, as path building, as commentary, as marking in or around existing text, as a decentering of authority, as a record of reading and interpretation, or as community memory.

  If you are a digital mark-maker, try pen and Bible. If you are a pen and Bible margin-writer, try online marking. What do you learn from this alternative way of working the margins?

- What would a "luminous" life look like for you? Read one of these Bible verses about luminous lives and illuminate that text in your margin:

2 Samuel 22:29	Job 33:28	Psalm 4:6
John 1:3-5	Matthew 5:16	John 8:12

- Watch Makoto Fujimura create painting from the biblical text: http://www.makotofujimura.com/four-holy-gospels/ How does his process of illumination inform your margins?

WRITING, TO SET THINGS RIGHT

The marginalia are deliberately penciled, because the mind
of the reader wishes to unburden itself of a thought. . . . In the marginalia
we talk only to ourselves; we therefore talk frankly, boldly, originally, with
abandonment, without conceit. . . . The circumscription of space in these
pencilings, has in it something more of advantage than inconvenience. It
compels us.

—*Edgar Allan Poe*

In scripture, we learn that margins help us to adjust a broken world. The margin of sabbath, the border of a field, the edge between neighbor and self; all work to set things right. This is the beauty of Leviticus 23 and the encouragement to mark the edges of the field for the one in need.

Ruth and Naomi found themselves in need and grateful for the edges of a field after the death of Ruth's husband, Naomi's son, left them destitute. Ruth went to the edge of Boaz's field and collected sheaves of wheat (Ruth 2:2). The margin Boaz left for them fed their hunger, met their need, and offered a first deed to set things right in their broken world. For Boaz, there was no difference between word and deed. Boaz knew that God's word transformed into action and that marginal practice mattered. In this journey through the margins, I hope you have gleaned just the wheat you need from the fields of your Bible and from the harvest of others.

In scripture, we learn that the margins are often a place where God writes love letters. And, the margins are a place where we learn how to love.

When Karl Barth encouraged the spiritual discipline of having the Bible in one hand and the newspaper in another, he hoped such a posture of prayer might set things right in a broken world. This is the same hope for writing in the margins, so that with Bible in one hand and pen in the other, our hearts and minds are realigned to serve boldly in a broken world. This scriptural practice is not about us reading the Bible, but as Barth would say, the Bible reads us. He said, "The Bible unfolds to us as we are met, guided, drawn on, and made to grow by the grace of God."

Words Do Things

Frederick Buechner tells us that words "do" things. He says it this way:

> In Hebrew the term *dabar* means both "word" and "deed."
> Thus to say something is to do something.
> "I love you." "I hate you." "I forgive you." "I am afraid."
> Who knows what such words do, but whatever it is, it can never be undone.

Words do things. The scripture text on the page works on us. The words of our culture and our lives work on us, for better or worse. In the margins, those two disparate worlds come together—for a moment—for a conversation to unfold. Something hidden—in the heart, in a part of the text otherwise lost to us—is revealed. From the power of those words released, things happen. Worlds change. New life is created. We are made right.

What's wonderful about the margins is their latent potential for discovery, creativity, and daily joy. The margins offer a place for faith to develop in clarity and deepen in mystery. The margins offer a place for hope to gain security, grace to gain awareness, and wisdom to find its ground. The margins are a place for love to be nurtured into actuality.

In the margins, conversations as profound as, "I love you," "I hate you," "I forgive you," "I am deeply afraid" can occur between God and us as we work out our relationships with one another.

Why do you write in the margins of your Bible? Is there a relationship you are trying to heal? Are there mysteries about God you hope to live into? Is there a loved one whose Bible you treasure as much for the margins as for the text?

Margins matter. They matter to me because seven words in the margin changed my life. The margins matter because I read page 999 of Rich's Bible shortly after his death. The margins matter because Rachel knows her father's love secured by one word on the page. The margins matter because you have a margin story I hope you will share. The margins matter because so much possibility exists in what remains to be written.

In a world all too divided, I wonder if the margins help to get us on the same page. Here, we discern meaning for our lives and we learn how to fall in love with God and with neighbor.

You see, what is amazing about the margins is that God in the very beginning of creation wrote into the margins. From the very beginning, the Lord God leans over and scribbles into our margins his very name so we might stay awake, so we might

WHEN GOD MADE the WORLD WAKE UP!

listen and see, so we might know what is good and right and just and true.

On that steamy, sleepy day when God made the world wake up, God wrote God's own name into the margins from antelopes to zebras. Sometimes God scribbles the tail of a star falling across the margin of the sky. Sometimes God writes God's very name Yahweh, I am what I am, Jehovah, Elohim into the margins of our memories. Sometimes God dictates in the marginal places where we question God's goodness, the simple word God spoke at creation over and over again, "Good."

God looks at the margins and sees possibility. Isn't it God who writes "Abba" in the margins reminding them for those moments when it's so easy to forget?

And, the beauty of God's script is that we are invited to do the same when we turn to scripture. Revelation? Write it down. Confession? Name it. Adoration? Offer thanks. Supplication? What grace do you need supplied for this day? Intercession? Tell me the cares of your heart, the people and places that need my attention today, tell me their names. So, God leans over and writes the name that reveals the deepest of relationships.

And we get to lean over and scribble our names as well. Rachel. Daniel. Leah. Jason. Caitlyn. Ed. Meghan. Jessica. Katie. Jennifer. Rich.

Katie Gordon understands that her dad discovered something in the margins that gave him peace. Katie, just eleven when Rich died, has not yet taken a look at his margins. She is waiting for that moment when the time is just right. She explains it this way,

> Growing up, I knew my dad had kept a special Bible next to his bed that he read it every day. It wasn't until after he died that I learned of him writing in the margins. To this day, I haven't read through it. Maybe it's because I'm not ready to have a look into his thoughts on life and what passages meant the most to him. Or maybe it's because I'm waiting for the right moment. I know that it

Rachel. Daniel Leah JASON Caitlyn ED Meghan Jessica KATIE Jennifer RICH

will be hard reading it, seeing as it meant so much to him but I'm
excited for the day when I can sit down and connect with my dad
again through the margins of his Bible.

Words Set Things Right

I am grateful to Rich, who shared his margins with me even in his death, so I could learn the power and the grace and the hope of this conversation. His margins are full of mysteries, prayers, and moments of revelation. For a lifetime, his family will understand his heart of prayer through the words on the page. In the margins, Rich learned how to fall in love—with God, with his enemies, with the hard parts of himself, with those closest to him.

On April 4, 2002, next to Genesis 46:3, Rich wrote, "I thought I was told my plan—to make someone else great." While his note denotes some skepticism, for each person reading this book, I think we all agree. Rich, you have.

Colossians 3:16 prays that the word of Christ might live in us richly. Margin writing deepens and expands, multiplies and makes possible the ways the words of Christ might dwell in our hearts and minds and souls.

The space around the page, that golden canon that is an incredible circle of light, offers a luminous place to engage the transcendent God. Here is a circle of blessing, a place of possibility wherein what is otherwise askew in your life and the world, might be made right as a divine conversation unfolds. This is the place for a gracious conversation, where the polyvalent layers of meaning in the text meet the many layers of meaning in your life and offer truth and guidance.

Too often we try and justify ourselves by our deeds or our desires. Christ longs to set things right within us as we come to understand his words of life for our own contexts. The margins are a place to work out

...here is a circle of blessing, a place of possibility

CIRCLE
of
BLESSING

that justification and to live into sanctification—lives lived wholly and holy as a gifted response to the great gift we find in Christ himself. *May the word of Christ dwell in you richly* is a text offering an incredible gift and joyous hope. Things will change as that word works within us, and that is good news. Words do things. Words set things right.

That "rightness" is more than confession, more than justification, more even than salvation. What is set right in the margins is the love of God made present to us through the whole salvation history from the Creation to the Resurrection.

The Word Shows Us How to Love

When Joyce Maynard, a famous author, was asked what is the most cherished book she owns, she lamented the singular book she wishes she had, but does not:

> *I could have purchased my own Bible of course. But it wasn't simply the Bible I wanted. It was my father's voice, speaking to me, his only Chum, from those oft-thumbed pages, and offering up his vision of what mattered in this life—as he had all those years when I'd taken his voice so for granted, and, too often, registered only impatience and annoyance with what he said.*

> *And here I am. Close to three decades have passed since my father died, but he remains a daily presence and only in part because the walls of the house I live in are covered with the art he made. In my fifties now, I wonder: Which were the Psalms he loved best? Which disciples? What were the stories he underlined, and the comments he would have written beside them in the margins in his fine, elegant artist's hand?*

Heart. Voice. The pages of scripture keep company with the communion of saints. Scripture as a "living" word takes on new meaning when we understand the impact of those who have loved scripture and shared that love with others. Where human love falters, the love of God prevails. We lean into that love in the margins where we are caught and kept by a love too deep to name.

The hymn-writer Frederick Lehman recognized the inability to ever fully capture the love of God. The first stanza of his hymn expresses that deep truth, *the love of God is far greater than tongue or pen can ever tell.* The irony of this truth is that by picking up a pen we come closer to understanding that love of God:

> Could we with ink the ocean fill,
> And were the skies of parchment made,
> Were every stalk on earth a quill,
> And every man a scribe by trade;
> To write the love of God above
> Would drain the ocean dry;
> Nor could the scroll contain the whole,
> Though stretched from sky to sky.

Such meditations on the love of God have moved the hands of hermits, calligraphers, genealogists, theologians, musicians, poets, artists, teenagers, rebels, and ordinary folks like you and me. God's love is so abundant it spills out into the edges of the page and then, into the edges of our lives. Margin writing allows us to linger on that love so that we can pray without ceasing as we engage this scriptural discipline.

Words do things. Words set things right in a broken world. God's word reads us and realigns our deepest needs into God's gracious will.

In one of Rich's margin notes, he writes simply, "Jen, I love you." Above that he adds at a later date, "More than ever."

Later, Rich writes, "Today Jennifer Kreuz Gordon taught me how to love."

May your margin writing nurture that same love. May you be blessed by that sacred ring of light. May the words of Christ dwell in you richly. As you write in that edge, may the word of God set things right in your life as you read and pray and write.

Connecting with God

Suzanne T. Eller

One day a friend commented on how "inked up" my Bible was while pointing to the underlined words, comments, and prayers written beside scriptures.

"I don't write in my Bible in ink," she said. "I only write in pencil."

She explained that she had had a tough childhood. While growing up, there were many people in her life that had let her down. Eventually she let herself down, and it hurt not only her, but also her children and her marriage.

One day she picked up a Bible and started reading it. To her, many of the scriptures seemed harsh, and she assumed those that were hopeful were meant for someone else. As she read, she wrote down comments. She wrote down questions. She penciled in a picture of a broken heart next to one scripture.

Then, over time, those scriptures started to make sense. What once seemed harsh now seemed loving. "God wasn't trying to take anything away from me. He was trying to give me life," she said.

The more she read, the more she wrote in the margins of her Bible, but always in pencil. Question marks were erased and comments of gratefulness replaced them. Scriptures that once seemed written for others were claimed as her own. One day she erased the picture of the broken heart and penciled in an image of a new heart—one that was whole and beautiful.

In Revelation 21:4 we are assured that God "wipes" away old things. That word means "to erase." He is continually writing in the margins of our lives, erasing tears, and writing in joy. Mourning or sadness ebbs away as God gently writes in hope for tomorrow.

What we might see as permanent, God sees written in pencil.

On the Pages of Your Bible

- Read Revelation 21:4 and reflect on the text. What if in one place God "wipes" away the old and writes in the new in the margins? Write into your margin what would be erased and what might be written in by God's grace.

- Words "do" things. So much so, that God wants to write on our own hearts. Jeremiah 31:33 offers this,

  This is the covenant that I will make with the people of Israel after that time, declares the LORD. I will put my Instructions within them and engrave them on their hearts.

  Through your practice of margin writing what has been written on your heart? Write that in the margin next to Jeremiah 31:33.

- Leviticus 23 is an extended reflection on "margins." Go back to this chapter and write into the margin some of the effects of your marginal practices. How has your margin writing shaped your ability to "live in the margins"? How has each informed the other?

- The margins are certainly a sacred "ring of light," a circle of blessing around the biblical text. Consider that space a halo of sorts. Turn to any of these psalms, which are reflections on that light, and write a prayer of thanks for the radiance and sacred presence you have found in the margins.

Psalm 97:11	Psalm 89:15
Psalm 119:105	Psalm 119:130

ACKNOWLEDGMENTS

The Gordon family has shared generously Rich's story and Bible knowing he would be honored that his life continues to make a difference. For their deep belief in this project, I am so grateful. Rich would be honored to know his Bible came alongside the work of the Common English Bible translation.

This project began with a story shared on the *Faith and Leadership* online magazine of Duke Divinity School. Thank you to Sally Hicks and Jason Byassee for their encouragement to write. That thanksgiving continues with others who have nurtured the ministry of writing: Sheldon Sorge, Tammy Weins, Mary Louise McCullough, Don Ottenhoff, Eugene Peterson, Sari Fordham, Elisa Schneider, Carla Durand, David White, David Maxwell, Natalie Gott Vizuette, Gretchen Ziegenhals, Benjamin McNutt, Lil Copan, and Lauren Winner. To the communities of the Collegeville Institute and the Ecclesial Literature Project, the *Faith and Leadership* team, the folks at the *Call and Response* blog, and to the *On Scripture* team of Odyssey Networks including Mary Brown, Matt Skinner, and Karen Meberg—thank you for being stewards of writing that fosters the imagination and leadership development for the church.

Countless thanks to the Lilly Foundation for your bold and courageous commitment to the work of kindling the pastoral imagination and upholding the hard work of pastoral ministry. Taking a vow to steward the religious "imagination" is a bold and courageous move for a foundation. Thank you for your ongoing cultivation of an "educated and virtuous American citizenry" as well as your commitment to clergy renewal. Your grants have blessed and healed my life and the life of my family. Thank you.

I am grateful to a team of scholars who offered their robust wisdom to this project. Thank you to Scott T. Carroll who offered a trail of fascinating stories to pursue even while he was hard at work laying the foundation with Steve Green for the National Bible Museum to be opened on the Washington Mall in 2016. Additional thanks to:

David Spadafora, John D. Laing, Don Moore, Mary Auenson, David C. Lachman, MaeAnn Walters, and Holly Patrick.

For the editing and layout of this book, thank you to: Lil Copan, Mary Johannes, Katherine Johnston, Sonua Bohannon, and the CEB Editorial and Translation teams. Thank you to Lauren Winner for your editorial panache, which is just as incredible as your "Taboo" playing skills.

Several circles of friendships have offered blessing and guidance. Thank you to Kathrine, Katie, Sue, Lisa, Veronica, Mary, Kelly, Courtney, and Angela. Thank you to Valerie Moore Phillips for her telephone prayer. Thank you to John Magnuson and Olivia Sweeney. Thank you to Kim, Diana, and Elaine. Thank you Betsy, Susan, and Wendy. Thank you to Jessica Shelenberger, Karen Weichman, Debbie Boyd, and Zoe Brown. Thank you Mary Rodgers, Sarah Woolsey, Catherine Clasen Agnew, and Kate Blanchard. Thanks Fritz, Dave, Calvin, and Jack for your writing encouragement. For all others who offer prayer and support, thank you. Thanks to Gary Swanson and Katie Bittner.

Rich's legacy has been sustained by friends through the Impact Internship. A special thanks to Ed Movic. And thank you to the Impact interns: John, Steve, Maggie, Caitlin, and Vaughn.

For church communities who offer circles of strength, thank you to

Sardis Presbyterian Church, Nassau Presbyterian Church, Immanuel Presbyterian Church, New Wilmington Presbyterian Church, and The Presbyterian Church of West Middlesex. Also thanks to Fox Chapel Presbyterian Church, Woodlawn Presbyterian Church, First United Presbyterian Church in Guthrie, Westfield Presbyterian Church, and Highland Presbyterian Church. A special thanks to Tom Kort and Ralph Hawkins. And thank you to the community of faith at the New Castle City Rescue Mission.

Thank you to the circle of women at Collegeville this summer: Lisa Durkee, Melissa Wiginton, Christina Holder, Kathy Snider, Renee Aukeman Prymus, Julie Craig, Eileen Kinch, Susan Thomas, Sharon Miller, Susan Sink, and Mary van Balen.

Thank you to friends, professors, and colleagues in the Theology Department at Duquesne University and for their living into the Spiritan tradition that it is the Spirit who gives life.

I am blessed with a family who never lets a dream get pushed into the margins. For all their support, thank you to Lee and Deb Nichols, Lynn and Steve Dull, Warren and Cinda Hickman, Robert Nichols, Maureen and Gary Swanson, Brenda Hickman, Christina and Bob Strait, Agnes Nichols, Lonnie and Terry Bobo, Lynn and T. J. Kennedy, Sharon and Joe Pegararo, and Bette Grigg. And to my Aunt Lane Ducker and "Miss" Deborah Barkley who are just as family to me.

Thank you to the writing space provide by Mugsies Coffee Shop in New Wilmington and the Flying Pig Coffee Shop and the G.V. Barbee Library at Oak Island.

My husband Jason's wisdom underlies the deepest thoughts in these pages. For his true companionship I am profoundly thankful. He is a husband, pastor, and father who is always reaching into the margins to lift up, love, and bring laughter. Leah and Caitlyn, I may hold the Bible with two hands, but there is no better day than having your hands in mine as we walk through fall leaves in the Golden Kingdom as we walk, talk, and laugh, sharing insights about life and love and God.

Thank you to the lives represented in the pages of this book and for their willingness to share their stories in the hope that others might be inspired. They live out the truth of Parker Palmer's quotation. He said, "If you can't write a paragraph, write a line or a word. And if you can't do that on the page, write your truth with your life, which is far more important than any book. . . . Here too, of course, is a parallel with the life of faith. The faith journey is less about making a big leap of faith than it is about putting one faithless foot in front of the other, and doing it again and again. What happens as you walk that way is sometimes transformed by grace."

Finally, I am thankful for just that grace.

Please share your margin story by visiting this website: http://writing-in-the-margins.com/ Here you may share your story, learn from new stories, and share practices for scriptural disciplines of writing in the margins.

NOTES

Sacred Edges

p 13 Dirk Johnson, "Book Lovers Fear Dim Future for Notes in the Margins," *The New York Times*, February 20, 2011.

Love Letters

p 19 Alastair Jamieson, "Art Gallery Invites Visitors to Deface the Bible," *The Telegraph*, July 23, 2009.

pp 20, 23 Mortimer Adler, "How to Mark a Book," *The Saturday Review of Literature*, July 6, 1941.

p 25 http://www.plymouthbrethren.org/article/5263

Laying Out the Golden Ratio of Page Design

p 41 Robert Bringhurst, *Elements of Typographic Style* (Point Roberts, Wash.: Hartley & Marks, Publishers, 1997), 145.

p 44 Annie Dillard, *The Writing Life* (New York: Harper Perennial, 1990), 58–59.

Marginalia and Memos, Scholia and Scribbles

p 64 Maria Popova, "Oh, My Hand: Complaints Medieval Monks Scribbled in the Margins of Illuminated Manuscripts," *Lapham's Quarterly,* March 2012.

p 65 Free Library of Philadelphia, http://libwww.freelibrary.org/medievalman/Detail.cfm?imagetoZoom=mca0281542

p 67 Tim Coulson and Aurelio Malo, "Population Biology: Case of the Absent Lemmings," *Nature*, November 6, 2008. http://www.nature.com/nature/journal/v456/n7218/full/456043a.html

p 67 Lynn McDonald, *Collected Works of Florence Nightingale: Florence Nightingale's Spiritual Journey*, volume 2 (Waterloo, Ontario: Wilfred Laurier University Press, 2001), 106.

p 68 http://www.ancestorhunt.com/family_bible_records.htm

pp 68-69 http://www.macfound.org/fellows/24/

Connecting Word to World: Praying the Horizontal and the Vertical

p 76 Norman Vincent Peale, *The Tough-minded Optimist* (New York: Prentice Hall, 1961), 45.

p 76 Thanks to Colin Yuckman for this insight into Bible study.

p 79 Terry A. Veling, *Practical Theology: On Earth as It Is in Heaven* (Maryknoll, NY: Orbis Books, 2005), 54.

Praying in That Inch of Space

p 85 *The Book of Discipline of the United Methodist Church* (Nashville: The United Methodist Publishing House, 2004), 77.

p 87 Presbyterian Church (U.S.A.), *Book of Order* (Louisville: Office of the General Assembly, 2005), chapter 5.

p 88 St. Ignatius Loyola, http://www.ignatianspirituality.com/ignatian-prayer/the-examen/

Writing Through Conflict

p 95 Mary Karr, *Lit: A Memoir* (New York: HarperCollins, 2009), 382.

p 95 Ibid., 383–84

p 98 http://www.nomorelyrics.net/card_michael-lyrics/313563-scribbling_in_the_sand-lyrics.html

Practicing Scriptural Disciplines

p 106 http://philpringle.com/_blog/Phil_Pringle_Blog

p 107 http://philpringle.com/_blog/Phil_Pringle_Blog/post/Big_key_to_a_Big_life/

Living in the Margins

p 113 Gregory Boyle, *Tattoos on the Heart: The Power of Boundless Compassion* (New York: Free Press of Simon & Schuster, 2010), 190.

p 113 Ibid., 21.

p 114 http://newsweek.washingtonpost.com/onfaith/panelists/susan_brooks_thistlethwaite/2009/02/gods_batterers_when_religion_s.html

p 115 http://www.caregivegrow.org/Press/081411AmakaGaMcKenzie.pdf

p 115 To find out more about the McKenzie Noelle Wilson Foundation, please visit the website at www.caregivegrow.org, "like" on Facebook/caregivegrow, or e-mail info@caregivegrow.org.

Marginal Writing in a Digital Age

p 123 http://www.csdl.tamu.edu/~marshall/ht98-final.pdf

Writing, To Set Things Right

p 130 Karl Barth, "The Strange New World of the Bible," *The Word of God and the Word of Man,* trans. Douglas Horton (London: Hodder and Stoughton Ltd., 1928), 30.

p 130 Frederick Buechner, *Beyond Words: Daily Readings in the ABC's of Faith* (New York: HarperCollins, 2004), 413.

p 134 Sean Manning, ed., *Bound to Last: 30 Writers on Their Most Cherished Book* (Philadelphia: Da Capo Press, 2010), 39.

p 135 http://library.timelesstruths.org/music/The_Love_of_God/

Acknowledgments

p 141 Parker Palmer, "Taking Pen in Hand," *Christian Century,* September 7, 2010.

BIBLIOGRAPHY

Adler, Mortimer. *How to Read a Book.* New York, NY, Simon and Schuster, 1940.

Barth, Karl. "The Strange New World of the Bible." In *The Word of God and the Word of Man,* trans. Douglas Horton. London: Hodder and Stoughton Ltd., 1928.

Birkerts, Sven. *The Gutenberg Elegies: The Fate of Reading in an Electronic Age.* New York: NY, Faber and Faber, 1994.

Fee, Gordon D. and Douglas Stuart. *How to Read the Bible for All Its Worth.* Grand Rapids, MI. Zondervan, 1981.

Gardner, John P. Jr. and Elizabeth D. Gardner. *Bound in the Bible: Creating Your Family Legacy within the Word of God.* PCG Legacy, 2010.

Gomes, Peter J. *The Good Book: Reading the Bible with Mind and Heart.* San Francisco, HarperCollins, 1996.

Ironside, H. A. *Dr. Ironside's Bible: Notes & Quotes from the Margins.* Loizeaux, 1976.

Jackson, H. J. *Marginalia: Readers Writing in Books.* New Haven, CT: Yale University Press, 2002.

MacBeth, Sybil. *Praying in Color: Drawing a New Path to God.* Boston: Paraclete Press, 2007.

Peterson, Eugene. *Eat This Book: A Conversation in the Art of Spiritual Reading*. Grand Rapids, MI: Eerdmans, 2006.

Veling, Terry. *Living in the Margins*. Eugene, OR: Wipf & Stock Publishers, 2002.

———. Practical Theology: On Earth as It Is in Heaven. Maryknoll, NY: Orbis Books, 2005.

To share your margin story, or to read more stories and scriptural practices, visit:

http://writing-in-the-margins.com/

Organizations

To find out more about the McKenzie Noelle Wilson Foundation, please visit the website at www.caregivegrow.org, "like" on Facebook/caregivegrow or e-mail info@caregivegrow.org.

Blogs and Web Resources

http://www.biblereadingproject.com/

http://www.doorposts.com/blog/2012/06/12/loving-the-bible-in-a-hands-on-way/

http://dannycoleman.blogspot.com/

www.tsuzanneeller.com

donmooreswartales.com

http://www.ancestorhunt.com/family_bible_records.htm

For other fine books, visit AbingdonPress.com

___think___ on common ground.

___walk___ on common ground.

___teach___ on common ground.

___pray___ on common ground.

___live___ on common ground.

COMMON
ENGLISH
BIBLE

the best scholars too) to make sure it speaks
clear and true. Let's make it fresh. Vibrant. Real.
Let's build a translation on common ground.

CPSIA information can be obtained at www.ICGtesting.com
Printed in the USA
LVOW03s1358190715

446763LV00009B/63/P